THE MISSING MESSIAH STUDY GUIDE

TYNDALE
elevate™
ask. seek. find.

KYLE IDLEMAN
MARK E. MOORE
WITH VINCE ANTONUCCI

A SIX-SESSION STUDY ON ENCOUNTERING THE JESUS WE CAN NO LONGER IGNORE

THE MISSING MESSIAH

STUDY GUIDE

Visit Tyndale online at tyndale.com.

Visit Tyndale Christian Resources online at tyndalechristianresources.com.

Visit the authors online at kyleidleman.com and markmoore.org.

The Missing Messiah Study Guide: A Six-Session Study on Encountering the Jesus We Can No Longer Ignore

Interior design by Brandi Davis

Published in association with Don Gates of the literary agency The Gates Group; the-gates-group.com.

For information about special discounts for bulk purchases, please contact Tyndale House Publishers at csresponse@tyndale.com, or call 1-855-277-9400.

ISBN 979-8-4005-2555-1

Printed in the United States of America

32 31 30 29 28 27 26
7 6 5 4 3 2 1

CONTENTS

INTRODUCTION

WELCOME TO THE STUDY GUIDE FOR *THE MISSING MESSIAH*!

This study is designed to help you go deeper into God's Word as you read *The Missing Messiah* and reflect on what it means that Jesus is not only Savior but also Messiah and King. Throughout this journey, you'll discover how we often subconsciously reshape Jesus into someone familiar and comfortable and how life-changing it is to rediscover him as the true, promised King, as revealed in Scripture.

Many people believe in Jesus and admire him, yet they miss what early Christians understood so clearly: that calling Jesus *Messiah* isn't simply a religious label but a declaration of allegiance. This study will help you recover that meaning. You'll explore what Scripture says about the Messiah, how cultural assumptions have reshaped our understanding of Jesus, and how his life, death, and resurrection reveal him as King over every part of life.

You may be coming to this study with lots of years of following Jesus in your back pocket, or you may be approaching this topic with your share of questions. Maybe you're hoping to lead a group to go deeper with the true Jesus, or perhaps you accepted a friend's invitation to explore who Jesus is. Maybe you sense there's more to faith than private belief or spiritual comfort, or maybe you wonder if we've lost something vital in how we talk about Jesus today. No matter where you're coming from, you're invited to approach this journey with openness and curiosity. If you do, you will not only learn more about Jesus—you may begin to see him more clearly than ever before.

Our study will reveal how the story of the Messiah stretches from Genesis to Revelation, how Jesus fulfills our deepest hopes, and why the resurrection is not simply a beautiful ending but the coronation of the King. You'll see how Jesus exceeded expectations, how the church has sometimes reshaped him to fit cultural preferences, and what it truly means to follow him as Rabbi, Lord, and King.

HOW TO USE THIS STUDY

This guide is designed for a six-week experience. Each week includes group teaching and discussion, along with daily reflections intended to help you live out what you're learning in real and practical ways. Note that day 5 of each week is intended to be a catch-up day and give you space to reflect on what you've learned over the past few days. While walking through this guide together in community is especially powerful, it can also be used for personal devotion and growth.

This study is designed to work in three integrated ways:

- **The book:** Each week corresponds to specific chapters in *The Missing Messiah*. Read the specified chapters before your group session to lay the foundation for your conversation.
- **The video:** Each session includes a teaching video that introduces the week's theme and sets up the group discussion. Videos can be accessed at tyndale.life/redeem using the unique digital access code provided at the beginning of this book.
- **Personal study:** Each week includes five days of guided personal reflection. After each group session, work through

the reflection questions on your own. These daily studies will help you dig deeper into Scripture, examine your own assumptions about Jesus, and apply what you're learning to everyday life.

You can engage with this study in a group or on your own. If you're going through it independently, read the assigned chapters, watch the teaching video, reflect on the discussion questions, and complete the daily studies at your own pace.

This study is especially impactful in community. If you're going through it in a group, read the assigned chapters before each group meeting and gather weekly to watch the teaching video together, discuss the questions, and encourage one another as you work through the personal reflections during the week.

If you're leading a group, the "Note to Leaders" section provides guidance for facilitating group discussions.

FROM INFORMATION TO TRANSFORMATION

The Missing Messiah calls us back to an essential truth about Jesus: that he's not simply a spiritual accessory but the promised King. This study guide is intended to move you from information to transformation. On these pages, you will take the truths explored in the book and bring them into your daily life through reflection, discussion, and application. Whether you engage in this study on your own or with a group, you'll be challenged to examine where you may have unknowingly reshaped Jesus to fit your preferences and invited to rediscover him as he truly is—the Messiah who calls you to wholehearted allegiance.

As you walk through the next six weeks, may your understanding of Jesus grow deeper, your allegiance to him grow stronger, and your love for him grow richer. May you rediscover the Messiah—not a customized version shaped by culture but the true King who calls us to follow him with our whole lives. And may that rediscovery lead you to a renewed, vibrant, and life-shaping faith.

If you're working through this study with a group, please read chapters 1–3 of *The Missing Messiah* before your first group session.

NOTE TO LEADERS

Thank you for leading this study! Your role is vital in helping participants rediscover Jesus as the true Messiah and King. This guide is designed to make your job easier while creating space for meaningful conversation and personal growth.

SUGGESTED SESSION STRUCTURE

Note that the suggested group session time is 90 minutes.

- **Welcome and connect (approximately 10 minutes):** Use the "Connect" questions to help participants connect with one another and share insights from the previous week's personal study. This time builds community and sets the tone for authentic discussion.
- **Watch the video (approximately 25 minutes):** Play the teaching video for the session. Encourage participants to take notes using the space provided.

- **Group discussion (approximately 30–45 minutes):** Work through the "Discuss" questions together. You don't need to cover every question—select the ones that are most relevant for your group. Listen for how the Spirit is moving and allow the conversation to go deeper rather than rushing to cover everything.
- **Respond (approximately 5 minutes):** Give people a few minutes to answer the "Respond" questions on their own.
- **Closing, prayer, and preview (approximately 5–10 minutes):** Briefly preview the week's personal study and close in prayer. Encourage participants to read the assigned chapters and complete the daily reflections before the next session.

TIPS FOR LEADING WELL

- **Read ahead:** Complete the week's reading and personal study before the session so you can guide the discussion with confidence.
- **Create a safe space:** Encourage honesty and vulnerability. Not everyone will be in the same place spiritually—and that's okay.
- **Don't feel pressure to have all the answers:** Your role is to facilitate, not to be the expert. It's fine to say, "That's a great question—let's explore that together."
- **Watch the clock but hold it loosely:** Some conversations are worth extending. If you're running short on time, focus on fewer questions with greater depth.
- **Point people back to Scripture:** This study is rooted in God's Word. When questions arise, help the group discover answers in the biblical text.
- **Pray for your group:** Ask God to open hearts, challenge assumptions, and draw each person closer to Jesus as King.

WHAT YOUR GROUP WILL GAIN

By the end of this study, participants will have a deeper understanding of who Jesus truly is—not the watered-down version created by culture but the promised Messiah and King. They'll be equipped to examine their own beliefs, identify where they've reshaped Jesus, and respond to him with wholehearted allegiance. More than information, this study aims for transformation—a renewed faith that shapes every area of life.

SESSION 1

RECOVERING THE REAL MESSIAH

SESSION 1

GROUP STUDY

WELCOME

In 2012, the art world was shocked by the unveiling of a new version of the *Mona Lisa*, which some claimed had been painted by da Vinci himself. The portrait, resembling classical Renaissance style, had been displayed for decades. Experts gathered to determine whether it was the masterpiece some claimed it to be.

At first glance, everything seemed right. But under infrared analysis, experts discovered that the layering, pigmentation, and painting technique didn't match Leonardo da Vinci's. It wasn't a malicious forgery; it was simply a painting that resembled the original enough to be mistaken for it.

It looked like da Vinci. It honored da Vinci. It just *wasn't* da Vinci.[1]

Many of us have unknowingly done the same thing with Jesus.

We believe in him. We worship him. We pray in his name. But over time, we've added layers—cultural expectations, political assumptions, personal preferences, therapeutic comfort—and ended up with a Jesus who resembles the original yet misses his true identity.

A Jesus who blesses our lives but doesn't rule them.

A Jesus who comforts but doesn't command.

A Jesus who saves us from sin but not from self-sovereignty.

The real Messiah isn't just a personal Savior; he's a King. And kings don't exist to fit into our lives; they reorder them.

When Peter declared, "You are the Messiah, the Son of the living God" (Matthew 16:16), he wasn't making a statement of affection; he was pledging allegiance. *Messiah* wasn't a spiritual nickname but a royal title meaning "God's chosen King." The early church risked their lives not because Jesus made them feel forgiven but because he claimed the throne.

This week, as we look at who Jesus truly is, consider this question: Have you embraced the real Messiah or just a familiar imitation?

He's far more demanding than the Jesus we often prefer. But he's also far more glorious.

CONNECT

If any of your group members don't know each other, take a few minutes to introduce yourselves. Then discuss one or both of the following questions:

Why did you decide to join this study? What do you hope to learn?

Think of a time when you met someone in person and they were different from what you expected. What surprised you most?

WATCH

Watch the session 1 video together. *To access this video session, follow the instructions located at the front of this book.*

NOTES

DISCUSS

Discuss what you read this week and what you learned from the video by working through these questions.

1. Invite someone to read Matthew 16:13-17. Peter identifies Jesus as the Messiah, God's chosen King. What do you think Peter understood about this title that we often miss today? How might understanding this shift how we relate to Jesus?

2. The book describes how we've created a "Build-A-Jesus"—customizing him to fit our preferences rather than surrendering to his lordship. What are some common ways Christians today might unconsciously customize Jesus to avoid his more challenging teachings or demands?

3. Jesus said, "If any of you wants to be my follower, you must give up your own way, take up your cross daily, and follow me" (Luke 9:23, NLT). How does this radical call to discipleship contrast with our comfortable Christianity that asks little of us? What would it look like to "take up your cross daily" in your life?

4. Throughout history, people have distorted Jesus to support their agendas—from Crusaders to slave owners to prosperity preachers. What are the warning signs that we're reshaping Jesus in our own image rather than being reshaped by him? How can we guard against this in our own lives?

5. If someone asked you why it matters that Jesus is both Savior and Messiah, how would you answer?

RESPOND

In this session, we've confronted the difference between a Jesus shaped by our culture and the Messiah revealed in Scripture. Take a few minutes to reflect on how Jesus' kingship might reshape your priorities, decisions, and allegiances.

> Christ is the visible image of the invisible God.
> He existed before anything was created and is supreme over all creation,
> for through him God created everything
> in the heavenly realms and on earth.
> He made the things we can see
> and the things we can't see—
> such as thrones, kingdoms, rulers, and authorities in the unseen world.
> Everything was created through him and for him.
> He existed before anything else,
> and he holds all creation together.
> Christ is also the head of the church,
> which is his body.
> He is the beginning,
> supreme over all who rise from the dead.
> So he is first in everything.
> For God in all his fullness
> was pleased to live in Christ,
> and through him God reconciled
> everything to himself.
> He made peace with everything in heaven and on earth
> by means of Christ's blood on the cross.

COLOSSIANS 1:15-20, NLT

Paul describes Jesus as the Creator, sustainer, and head of the church. Which of these roles most stretches your understanding of who Jesus is? Why?

Paul says Jesus must be "supreme . . . in everything" (verse 18). What is one area of your life where Jesus is currently not supreme? What would change if he were?

PRAY

Close your time together in prayer.

- Thank Jesus not only for saving you but also for reigning over your life as King.
- Ask him to expose any places where you have shaped him into your own image and ask for courage to follow him as the true Messiah.
- Pray that your group would pursue allegiance, not just admiration, in the weeks ahead.

SESSION 1

PERSONAL STUDY

As we progress through the book, group discussions, and Bible studies, each week will build on the last, moving from recognizing the true Messiah to reshaping our lives around him.

Throughout this first week, we will explore what it truly means to know Jesus as the Messiah—not a customized version we've created but the revolutionary King revealed in Scripture. This week focuses on identity: who Jesus truly is and why getting that answer right changes everything else. Each day will help you think more deeply about how we've domesticated Jesus and what it means to follow him on his terms.

As you work through each of these exercises, make sure to write down your responses. (If you're engaging in this study as part of a group, you'll have a few minutes to share your insights at the start of the next session.)

DAY 1

WHEN WE MAKE JESUS IN OUR IMAGE

In the early 2010s, the *Oxford English Dictionary* added a secondary definition to the word *literally*: "used for emphasis while not being literally true."[2] In other words, *literally* could now officially mean . . . not literally. Why? Because widespread misuse ("I literally died laughing") became common enough that the dictionary adapted to popular usage rather than strictly adhering to the original meaning.

Language evolves, and sometimes that's harmless—even helpful. But when this happens with Jesus—when we redefine who he is based on how we prefer to see him—we end up with a version that contradicts the original.

"Jesus is love" becomes code for "Jesus approves of whatever I want to do."

"Jesus brings peace" becomes "Jesus wants me comfortable and undisturbed."

"Jesus saves" becomes "Jesus fixes my problems" rather than "Jesus rescues me from rebellion against God."

The real Jesus hasn't changed. But our cultural dictionary has redefined him into someone he never claimed to be.

That happens subtly.

Culture applies pressure—through politics, comfort, relationships, and personal desires—and it feels easier to reshape Jesus into a socially acceptable mascot rather than honor him as a sovereign King. We want the Jesus who heals, forgives, and helps us succeed but not the Jesus who overturns tables, confronts sin, rebukes pride, and calls us to die to ourselves.

The real Jesus doesn't come to agree with us—he comes to rule us.

He asserts unmatched authority: "All authority in heaven and on earth has been given to me" (Matthew 28:18).

He demands costly allegiance: "If any of you wants to be my follower, you must give up your own way, take up your cross daily, and follow me" (Luke 9:23, NLT).

And he warns that many will settle for a counterfeit: "These people honor me with their lips, but their hearts are far from me" (Matthew 15:8).

The question this study raises isn't whether Jesus loves us—he absolutely does. The question is whether we love the real him or merely a custom-built version that fits our preferences.

A Jesus who always agrees with you isn't your Savior—he's your reflection.

The real Messiah is worth following precisely because he confronts us. If he never challenges your values, priorities, or comfort, it may be a sign you've stopped following him and started following *you.*

Today is an invitation to let Jesus define Jesus—and to let him define us.

READ AND RESPOND

Read Matthew 28:18-20; Luke 9:23-26; Matthew 15:1-9.

1. Before Jesus ascended, he declared that all authority in heaven and on earth belonged to him. He commissioned his followers to make disciples of every nation. How does Jesus' claim of total authority challenge the way people often treat faith as optional or private?

2. In Luke 9:23-26, Jesus describes discipleship not as belief alone but as self-denial, daily surrender, and willingness to lose our lives for his sake. What specific comfort, habit, or priority might Jesus be calling you to surrender to follow him more fully?

3. Write down assumptions you hold about Jesus. Where might they come from (culture? upbringing? personal preference?)? What does the Bible *actually* say about Jesus?

My Assumption About Jesus	Where It Came From	What Scripture Actually Shows

4. In Matthew 15, Jesus rebukes the religious leaders for honoring God outwardly while resisting him inwardly, for keeping tradition but ignoring obedience. Where do you feel the tension between honoring Jesus publicly and obeying him privately in your own life?

5. What is one specific action you will take this week to follow Jesus as he truly is, not as you prefer him to be?

DAY 2

THE MESSIAH WHO CONFRONTS OUR ALLEGIANCES

While most of the world barely noticed, something remarkable happened in the Kingdom of Tonga: Some fifteen thousand Tongans traveled from across the globe in 2015, sacrificing time and expense to witness the coronation of King Tupou VI. As the newly crowned monarch proceeded through the streets of Nuku'alofa from church to palace, hundreds of schoolchildren sat for hours in the heat, dressed in traditional attire and seated on woven mats, creating a guard of honor for their sovereign. The celebration, rooted in rituals a thousand years old, lasted eleven days.[3]

They weren't celebrating a political figure; they were submitting to a king.

Westerners often struggle to identify with this concept because we relate to leadership through preference: We vote people into office, criticize them on social media, replace them when disappointed, and "follow" them only as long as it benefits us. Allegiance is conditional.

When Jesus arrives announcing, "The Kingdom of God is near," we tend to interpret him only as someone who is bringing something to help us, not as someone who is coming to reign over us.

But Scripture consistently presents Jesus not as a personal life coach but as the promised King who was foretold for centuries: "A child is born to us. . . . The government will rest on his shoulders" (Isaiah 9:6, NLT).

Jesus doesn't merely save us from sin—he calls us into his Kingdom, where his authority reshapes reality: "He has rescued us from the kingdom of darkness and transferred us into the Kingdom of his dear Son" (Colossians 1:13, NLT).

That's why the early church was persecuted—not for worshiping Jesus privately but for publicly declaring, "Jesus is Lord." In Rome, that phrase wasn't a religious catchphrase; it was treason. To claim Jesus as King was to say Caesar wasn't.

Today we don't face emperors, but we do face competing allegiances—career, family expectations, ideology, nationalism, self-autonomy. The question is no longer "Who is Caesar?" but "Who or what gets the final say in your life?"

Calling Jesus *Messiah* forces a choice: Will we worship the King who confronts us or the version of Jesus who agrees with us?

The real King doesn't fit into our priorities—he defines them. And that's not limiting; it's freeing. Because whatever sits on the throne of your life rules you, regardless. Better a King who loves you than a kingdom you must sustain.

READ AND RESPOND

Read Isaiah 9:6-7; Colossians 1:13-14; Philippians 2:9-11.

1. Isaiah prophesies about a coming King whose rule is eternal and whose government rests on his shoulders, not ours. How do these verses expand your view of what Jesus came to do beyond forgiving sins?

2. In Colossians 1, Paul describes salvation as a transfer of kingdoms—out of darkness and into the reign of Christ. How does thinking in terms of "kingdom transfer" change how you understand discipleship and obedience?

3. Which earthly loyalties most compete with Jesus' reign in your life (success, safety, approval, political identity, comfort, control)? Rank the top three and reflect briefly on the implications.

Competing Allegiance	How It Competes	What Surrender Might Look Like
1.		
2.		
3.		

4. In Philippians 2:9-11, Paul declares that every knee will bow to Jesus—not just as a private Savior but as cosmic Lord. What might it look like for a person to bow to Jesus now rather than later? What would it look like for *you*, today?

5. What is one intentional act of allegiance you will practice this week to acknowledge Jesus as King, not just Savior?

DAY 3

THE LONGING FOR THE REAL MESSIAH

In his book *Mere Christianity*, C. S. Lewis observed something profound: Every natural desire corresponds to something real. We feel hunger because food exists, fatigue because sleep exists, thirst because water exists. But there is another hunger: a longing for meaning, wholeness, justice, and transcendence that nothing in this world can fill. Lewis concluded that this desire points beyond the world itself: "If I find in myself a desire which no experience in this world can satisfy, the most probable explanation is that I was made for another world."[4]

Centuries earlier, Augustine reached a similar conclusion in *Confessions*, writing that human beings were created for God and therefore remain restless until they find their rest in him.[5] The human ache for fulfillment is not merely psychological—it's theological. We were designed to belong to the King.

We are drawn to stories of redemption, sacrifice, and rescue because they echo the story we were made for. This is why political movements promise hope, relationships promise completion, careers promise identity, and possessions promise security: All are counterfeit kings attempting to satisfy a messianic longing woven into our souls.

Yet every substitute eventually fails.

The people of Israel experienced this cycle repeatedly. They longed for a king who would rescue, rule, and restore them—and ended up disappointed whenever they trusted human rulers. Only when Jesus arrived did those ancient longings find their fulfillment: "I, the Lord, will rule from Jerusalem as their king forever" (Micah 4:7, NLT).

Jesus doesn't simply answer spiritual questions; he satisfies spiritual hunger. He is not one option among many; he's the one every other hope imitates but can't match. He satisfies us not only by comforting us but by reorienting our deepest desires. The Messiah doesn't just fill our hunger; he reshapes what we hunger for.

This explains why following Jesus often feels like surrender rather than self-fulfillment. The path to satisfaction is not self-expression—it's allegiance.

Our souls were not designed to thrive under autonomy but under a good King.

The question is not whether you worship something; it's whether what you worship can bear the weight of your soul.

Only the real Messiah can.

READ AND RESPOND

Read Micah 4:6-8; Psalm 42:1-2; John 6:35-40.

1. In Micah's prophecy, God promises a future Kingdom where he himself reigns over his people. How does this vision of God as King speak to the deep longings people carry—longings for justice, security, and belonging?

2. In Psalm 42, David describes his soul longing for God like a deer thirsting for water. When have you felt a deep spiritual longing? What were you seeking at the time, and did you recognize it as hunger for God?

3. Where do you find yourself seeking ultimate satisfaction? Put an *X* in the spot that best represents your current reality.

Worldly Solutions ——————————————— Jesus as Messiah

What might help you shift more toward "Jesus as Messiah"?

4. Jesus calls himself the "bread of life," promising satisfaction only he can provide (John 6:35). Based on this passage, how does Jesus satisfy us in ways people, success, achievement, and control can't?

5. What is one longing or emotional need you're currently looking to fill elsewhere that you will bring to Jesus this week? What would it look like for you to seek to have it fulfilled in him?

DAY 4

REPRESENTING THE REAL MESSIAH TO THE WORLD

A 2020 survey of more than three thousand people in the United Kingdom found that 71 percent edit their selfies before posting them on social media. Only 29 percent would post an unedited photo. The changes are usually subtle—adjusting lighting, smoothing skin, whitening teeth, slimming a face. Apps like Facetune, downloaded tens of millions of times, make professional-level retouching available to anyone with a smartphone.[6] A 2021 study found that the vast majority of young women reported using filters or editing tools to even out skin tone, reshape facial features, or adjust body proportions before posting.[7]

The motivation is understandable. When most people assume others are posting edited images, the pressure to keep up is real. People are presenting their most carefully curated selves.

Over time, this cycle of editing reshapes what we believe is normal, achievable, and true. When everyone presents a filtered version of themselves, reality itself becomes distorted.

Many Christians do something similar . . . with Jesus.

We present a filtered version of Christ to the world. We emphasize his love but edit out his lordship. We highlight his comfort while downplaying his commands. We showcase his acceptance and minimize his call to repentance. Slowly, we adjust his image until it feels safe, familiar, and culturally acceptable.

The result? We become ambassadors of a Jesus who looks right—but isn't fully real.

A Jesus who affirms without transforming.

A Jesus who comforts without confronting.

A Jesus who fits neatly into culture rather than challenging it.

Paul reminds us that we are Christ's ambassadors (see 2 Corinthians 5:20). Ambassadors don't edit the message to make it palatable. They represent their King faithfully, even when the unfiltered truth is uncomfortable.

The danger isn't just that we misunderstand Jesus ourselves—it's that we misrepresent him to a watching world. A filtered Christ may be easier to accept, but he lacks the power to transform.

The real Messiah doesn't need our filters. He calls us to represent him as he truly is—because only the unedited Jesus can truly change lives.

READ AND RESPOND

Read 2 Corinthians 5:17-21; 1 Peter 2:9-12; Matthew 5:13-16.

1. In 2 Corinthians 5, Paul says followers of Jesus are new creations and ambassadors of reconciliation. What does representing Jesus as an ambassador require beyond simply believing in him?

2. Paul calls us ambassadors, which means we deliver the message of the one we represent, not our own. If you were to honestly assess yourself, are you more tempted to add things to Jesus' message or to subtract difficult parts? What are you tempted to add or subtract? Why do you think that is?

3. Peter describes believers as a "royal priesthood" meant to declare God's goodness to the world (1 Peter 2:9). According to this passage, how does our holy living play a role in how others see Jesus?

4. How would others describe Jesus from watching your life?

   Based on my words:

   Based on my actions:

   Based on my priorities:

   What needs to change to give a clearer picture?

5. In Matthew 5, Jesus calls his followers salt and light—visible and distinct in the world. What is one environment where you will intentionally represent the real Jesus this week? What will you do differently to represent him more accurately?

DAY 5

WRAP-UP

Use this time to go back and complete any of the study and reflection questions from previous days that you were unable to finish. Make a note of any revelations you've had and reflect on any growth or personal insights you've gained.

Read chapters 4–5 in *The Missing Messiah* before the next group session. Use the space provided to make note of anything in those chapters that stands out to you or encourages you.

SESSION 2

THE MORPHING MESSIAH

SESSION 2

GROUP STUDY

WELCOME

In 1519, Spanish conquistador Hernán Cortés landed in Mexico with fewer than six hundred men and sixteen horses. He faced the Aztec Empire—millions of people, a strong army, and a thriving civilization. By any reasonable measure, the Aztecs should have wiped out this small group of foreigners. Instead, within two years, the Aztec Empire had fallen.

The Spanish conquest succeeded for many reasons, but one might surprise you: translation.

Cortés depended on two interpreters. Jerónimo de Aguilar spoke Spanish and Mayan. La Malinche spoke Mayan and Nahuatl, the language of the Aztecs. In the early months, every message passed through two translators and three languages before reaching Montezuma II, the Aztec ruler. With each step, meaning shifted.[1]

When Cortés and Montezuma finally met face-to-face in November 1519, Malinche served as the primary interpreter. Montezuma delivered a speech in Tecpillahtolli, a formal style of Nahuatl used by nobility, known for indirect language and reverential speech.

The Spanish interpreted his words as submission. That was not what Montezuma intended.

The problem was not a single mistranslated word; it was a clash of worlds.

Spanish ideas of kingship, divinity, and tribute did not line up with Aztec concepts of power and honor. What the Aztecs meant as ceremonial courtesy, the Spanish heard as surrender. When language failed to carry full meaning, assumptions rushed in to fill the gaps.[2]

The tragedy was confidence without clarity (or possibly even willful misunderstanding).

Something similar happened with Jesus.

As the gospel moved from Hebrew to Greek, from Jerusalem to Athens, from Jewish communities to Gentile ones, the word *Messiah* was translated into *Christ*. The words matched, but the meaning shifted. The Hebrew word (*Messiah*) carried generations of Jewish hope—promises of God's Kingdom, dreams of restoration, echoes of David's throne. The Greek word (*Christ*) gradually became shifted away from that story, reshaped by Greek philosophy and Roman power.

The shift was not intentional; it was inevitable. Every language carries a worldview. Every translation involves interpretation. The question is not whether culture has shaped how we understand Jesus—it has. The deeper question is whether something essential has been lost along the way.

Have we kept the name but missed the King?

This week, we will explore how Western culture has influenced our understanding of Jesus to help us recognize the lenses we bring to Scripture.

CONNECT

What spoke to you from last week's personal study that you'd like to share with the group?

What comes to mind when you hear the word *Christ*? How is that different from what first-century Jews would have thought when they heard *Messiah*?

WATCH

Watch the session 2 video together. *To access this video session, follow the instructions located at the front of this book.*

NOTES

DISCUSS

1. Invite someone to read Colossians 2:8. Paul warns against being shaped by human ideas rather than by Christ. In what ways do you see cultural beliefs or traditions influencing how people think about Jesus today? How can we tell the difference between showing Jesus' relevance in our culture and reshaping Jesus to fit our culture?

2. The book explains that *Christ* means "Anointed One." It's not Jesus' last name. What changes when we remember that Jesus is King, not just a Savior from sin or a personal spiritual guide?

3. Western culture often frames faith as a private, personal relationship with Jesus. What parts of Jesus' mission are overlooked when we treat faith as only individual and personal? What can we learn from the early church about living out faith together?

4. Invite someone to read Acts 17:22-31. Paul connected with his audience's ideas but still challenged their assumptions. What does this passage teach us about sharing Jesus in a culture that thinks differently from the way we think?

5. The book describes how WEIRD culture (**W**estern, **E**ducated, **I**ndustrialized, **R**ich, **D**emocratic) shapes our faith. Which part of that culture do you think most influences—or distorts—the way we see Jesus? What's one practical way we can become more aware of those blind spots?

RESPOND

We've explored how cultural assumptions can morph our understanding of the Messiah. Take a few minutes on your own to examine what cultural filters might be shaping your view of Jesus.

> Don't copy the behavior and customs of this world, but let God transform you into a new person by changing the way you think. Then you will learn to know God's will for you, which is good and pleasing and perfect.
>
> **ROMANS 12:2, NLT**

Paul urges believers to be transformed in how they think rather than being shaped by the world around them. What's one cultural value that has influenced how you think about Jesus? What might it look like for God to renew your thinking in that area?

When you look at Jesus as he's revealed in Scripture, what's one aspect of his character or what he calls us to that you tend to downplay or avoid? Consider one concrete step you could take this week to respond to that part of him more seriously.

PRAY

Close your time together in prayer.

- Pray for the discernment to recognize where cultural assumptions have morphed your understanding of Jesus.
- Ask the Holy Spirit to reveal blind spots created by living in our WEIRD culture.
- Pray for humility to admit that your grasp of who Jesus is may be incomplete or distorted by cultural filters.
- Ask God to renew your mind and transform you so you're following the true Messiah, not a culturally customized version.
- Pray for wisdom to distinguish between faithful contextualization and cultural captivity, and ask for courage to follow Jesus on his terms rather than your culture's terms.

SESSION 2

PERSONAL STUDY

Throughout this week, we'll examine how cultural assumptions can reshape our understanding of Jesus. Each day will help you recognize the difference between faithfully contextualizing the gospel and allowing culture to morph the Messiah into something he never claimed to be. This week focuses on culture—and how, if we're not careful, our social, political, and personal assumptions quietly reshape our understanding of the Messiah.

As you work through these exercises, write down your honest responses. (If you're engaging in this study as part of a group, you'll have a few minutes to share your insights at the start of the next session.)

DAY 1

LOST IN TRANSLATION

Sometimes the problem is not what you're saying; it's what people are hearing.

One famous story about this principle goes like this: In the 1970s, Chevrolet introduced the Nova to Latin American markets with great excitement. The car had sold well in the United States, and executives expected the same success elsewhere. It never came—sales were terrible. Eventually someone made a connection. In Spanish, *no va* sounds like "doesn't go." It seems difficult to sell a car whose name is reminiscent of "It doesn't work."

Translation mistakes can be funny. They can also be costly. And while this example may be more myth than reality, it's not uncommon for the truth to be lost in translation.[3]

When KFC entered China, its slogan, "Finger-lickin' good," was translated as "Eat your fingers off." Pepsi promised to help customers "Come alive," but the message landed as "Pepsi brings your ancestors back from the grave." The words were close. The meaning was not. Every language carries hidden assumptions that seem obvious to insiders and confusing to everyone else.[4]

Something similar happened when the gospel moved from Hebrew into Greek.

The Hebrew word for Messiah was translated as *Christos*, or Christ. On the surface, the translation works. Both mean "Anointed One." But words are never just their definitions. They carry history. They carry hope. They carry expectations.

When first-century Jews heard *Messiah*, they thought of David's throne, national restoration, God's promises, and God's Kingdom breaking into the world. When Greeks heard *Christ*, they heard something more like a title.

This was not intentional distortion. The early church faced an enormous challenge. How do you explain a Jewish Messiah to people who have never read Israel's Scriptures? How do you preach a crucified King to a culture that sees crucifixion as shameful and absurd? Paul and the early believers had to translate the gospel not only into new languages but into new ways of thinking.

When *Messiah* became *Christ*, some precious implications slipped to the back burner. The weight of prophecy. The shock of a true King. The claim that God's Kingdom was confronting Caesar's empire. Eventually, the title *Christ* functioned almost like a last name. Jesus Christ sounded no more disruptive than Bob Smith. A title became familiar. A revolution became respectable.

We still feel the effects.

When we forget that *Christ* means "the anointed King," faith loses its edge. We assume we can believe in Christ while pledging loyalty to a rival King. We try to worship Christ without seeing that his Kingdom challenges every other kingdom.

When meaning fades, we don't just misunderstand a word—we miss the invitation to live under a very different King.

READ AND RESPOND

Read Matthew 16:13-20; Acts 2:36; 1 Corinthians 1:22-25.

1. When Peter said, "You are the Messiah," he was recognizing Jesus as God's promised King (Matthew 16:16). Jesus called this revelation foundational. Why do you think recognizing Jesus as Messiah—God's chosen King—is central to Christian faith?

2. How does it change things when *Christ* is understood as a claim about who Jesus is, not just part of his name?

3 At Pentecost, Peter declared that Jesus is "both Lord and Messiah" in a city ruled by Rome—a dangerous claim (Acts 2:36). How does this reshape the way you think about following Jesus? What might it look like to live under Jesus' kingship in your everyday decisions?

4. Compare these two ways of understanding *Christ*:

   Understanding 1: "Christ is Jesus' last name—it's basically just what we call him or how we identify him."

   Understanding 2: "Christ means 'the anointed King'—it's a revolutionary claim that he is the rightful ruler whose Kingdom trumps all earthly kingdoms."

   Write down how each understanding will lead to different ways of following Jesus.

5. In 1 Corinthians 1, Paul says "Christ crucified" didn't fit Jewish or Greek expectations—it offended both cultures. What parts of the real Messiah feel uncomfortable or challenging in today's cultural climate?

6. What's one area of your life where you sense Jesus inviting you to follow him more as King than as someone who simply agrees with you?

DAY 2

THE INDIVIDUALISM TRAP

In 1984, Apple Computer aired a Super Bowl commercial that became iconic. Directed by Ridley Scott, the ad showed gray-clad drones marching in unison toward a giant screen, where Big Brother preached conformity. A lone runner burst onto the scene and hurled a hammer, shattering the image. The closing line was simple and bold: "1984 won't be like *1984*." Apple cast itself as a symbol of freedom—the individual standing against the system.[5]

That commercial captured something essential about Western culture. We believe individuals matter more than groups. We value personal freedom over communal obligation. We celebrate the lone hero, the rebel, the self-made person who resists the crowd. Much of our society is built on protecting individual rights, expanding personal choice, and encouraging self-expression.

This emphasis is not entirely wrong. Scripture affirms individual dignity and personal responsibility. Jesus knows his sheep by name. He gave his life for real people, not an abstract mass (see John 10:14-15, 25-26). Yet Western Christianity has absorbed so much individualism that we've lost something essential about what it means to follow the Messiah together.

Think of how we talk about faith: "Do you have a personal relationship with Jesus?" "Have you accepted Jesus as your personal Savior?" "What is God doing in your life?" These are not bad questions, but they frame faith almost entirely around individual experience. Christianity becomes about me and Jesus—*my* salvation, *my* growth, *my* story—while the community fades into the background.

The early Christians would have found this strange. When Peter preached at Pentecost, thousands believed and immediately formed a community. They devoted themselves to shared teaching, shared meals, shared prayer, and shared lives (see Acts 2:40-47). Faith was personal but never private. To be saved meant joining a family and becoming part of a body.

Jesus called disciples, not independent followers. He sent them out together, not alone. He prayed for their unity, not just their individual maturity. Even when he taught them to pray, he used plural language: "Give *us* this day *our* daily bread" (Matthew 6:11, KJV, emphasis added). Following Jesus was always meant to be communal.

The danger of extreme individualism is not only loneliness; it's misunderstanding the Kingdom Jesus came to bring. His Kingdom is not a loose collection of believers who happen to agree. It is a new people, shaped together under his reign. We can't follow a King in isolation. Kings have kingdoms, and kingdoms are communal by nature.

READ AND RESPOND

Read Acts 2:42-47; 1 Corinthians 12:12-27; Ephesians 4:11-16.

1. Luke describes the early church as sharing life together—learning, eating, praying. How does this picture challenge the "me and Jesus" version of faith that's common today? What might shared Christian life look like in your own context?

2. Paul describes the church as one body made up of many parts that need each other. Where do you find it hardest to depend on other believers—or to let them depend on you?

3. Mark where you see yourself on this continuum:

Faith is primarily *individual* ———————— Faith is primarily *communal*

What experiences or influences have shaped that view?

What might a healthier balance look like for you?

4. In Ephesians 4, Paul says spiritual gifts are given to build up the church, not just the individual. How does that challenge the idea that our strengths exist mainly for our success, personal growth, and personal fulfillment?

5. What's one practical step you could take this week to move toward a more shared, communal faith? What might you need to rearrange—or give up—to do that?

DAY 3

THE WEIRD TEST

In the 1950s, psychologist Leon Festinger studied a doomsday cult that believed aliens would rescue them before Earth's destruction. When the predicted apocalypse didn't happen, Festinger expected the group to abandon its beliefs and disband. Instead, they doubled down, claiming their faith had saved the world. Festinger identified this as "cognitive dissonance"—the tendency to reinterpret reality when facts threaten deeply held beliefs.[6]

That same bias can impact our discipleship.

We can intellectually agree that **W**estern, **E**ducated, **I**ndustrialized, **R**ich, **D**emocratic (WEIRD) culture distorts our view of Jesus while practically living as if this doesn't affect us personally. It's like nodding along to a sermon about materialism while mentally planning your next Amazon order.

Let's move from agreement to self-examination by doing a diagnostic test to expose how our culture might be shaping our discipleship:

The Individualism Test: When you read Jesus' teachings, like in the Sermon on the Mount, do you instinctively think, *What does this mean for me?* or *What does this mean for us as God's people?* If your first instinct is always "me," that's WEIRD individualism. When Jesus said, "You are the light of the world," he used the plural form of *you*—he was talking to the community, not just individuals (Matthew 5:14).

The Intellectualism Test: When you last studied the Bible, did you read it alone for head knowledge or with others to obey it together? WEIRD culture says spiritual maturity comes through academic Bible study. The early church emphasized learning Scripture in community and practicing it corporately. Both methods are important for different purposes.

The Compartmentalization Test: How much of your week is "secular" versus "sacred"? Do you have "work life" that's separate from your "spiritual life"? Would your coworkers be surprised to learn you're a Christian? First-century disciples didn't clock in and out of following Jesus. He was Lord of everything—meals, money, work, rest, relationships.

The Self-Reliance Test: When did you last genuinely depend on God for something you couldn't control? WEIRD wealth insulates us. We have savings accounts (we don't need daily bread), we have health insurance (we don't need healing), we have 401(k)s (we don't need to trust God for our future). We've tried to eliminate dependence.

The Consumerism Test: Have you church-shopped? Have you ever thought, *I'm not being fed there* or *That worship style isn't my thing*? It's a symptom of WEIRD democracy when we treat church like a buffet. The early church was a messy, committed family. People stayed and learned to love because that's what the Kingdom requires.

Following the real Messiah requires different habits: communal rather than individual, embodied rather than intellectual, integrated rather than compartmentalized, dependent rather than self-reliant, submitted rather than entitled.

You can't fully escape WEIRD culture. But you *can* recognize it, resist it, and replace it.

READ AND RESPOND

Read Matthew 6:19-24; Romans 12:1-8; James 2:14-17.

1. Which test convicted you most? Where are you most WEIRD in your approach to Jesus?

    - ☐ Individualism
    - ☐ Intellectualism
    - ☐ Compartmentalization
    - ☐ Self-reliance
    - ☐ Consumerism

2. Jesus says in Matthew 6:24 that no one can serve both God and money. Where do you feel tension between trusting God and protecting financial security? What specific choice this week would demonstrate allegiance to God's Kingdom?

3. Romans 12 describes believers as members of one body, not independent entities. How does this image challenge the way you currently approach church, your commitments, and your responsibility to others?

4. James insists that faith without action is dead. Identify one teaching of Jesus you understand well but rarely practice. What keeps that teaching from shaping your daily behavior?

5. Choose one concrete step this week to move from a WEIRD habit toward biblical discipleship:

   - ☐ Less individual, more communal: Read Scripture with someone and discuss it together.
   - ☐ Less intellectual, more embodied: Pick one teaching of Jesus and do it without analyzing first.
   - ☐ Less compartmentalized, more integrated: Bring Jesus into a "secular" space (work, finances, neighborhood).
   - ☐ Less self-reliant, more dependent: Give away something you're holding for security.
   - ☐ Less consumer, more committed: Serve in your church in an area you don't prefer.

   What will you do, and when will you do it?

DAY 4

RECOVERING THE REAL MESSIAH

In a small church in Borja, Spain, a faded fresco of Jesus was once displayed quietly on the wall. Painted in 1930 by Elías García Martínez, the artwork—titled *Ecce Homo*, meaning "Behold the Man"—depicted Jesus crowned with thorns. Over the decades, the image slowly deteriorated.

In 2012, an elderly parishioner named Cecilia Giménez decided to help. She loved the church. She cared deeply about the image of Jesus. Though she had no training in art restoration, she carefully applied paint, layer by layer, believing she was restoring what time had damaged.

When the work was revealed, the response was immediate and brutal. Jesus' face was barely recognizable. His features were blurred and distorted. The crown of thorns looked like a smudge. The media quickly dubbed it "Monkey Jesus." Giménez was heartbroken. She believed she had been faithful to the original; in reality, she had transformed it into something else entirely.[7]

With good intentions and sincere devotion, she created a distortion instead of restoring the truth.

We have often done the same with Jesus.

Over time, cultures have added layers to his image. Jewish Christianity gave way to Greek understandings. Medieval theology shaped faith in one direction, the Reformation in another. Enlightenment thinking emphasized reason. Therapeutic culture can soften Jesus into a source of comfort. Nationalism recasts him as a symbol of power. Each generation believes it's being faithful. Each added layer slowly obscures the original portrait.

How do we recover the real Messiah? Not by pretending we can escape culture—that's impossible. We are all shaped by our context, just as the first Christians were shaped by theirs. But we can do what skilled restorers do: We can return to the original source. We can study the earliest witnesses. We can compare later interpretations to the first evidence. With humility and care, we can remove what distorts.

For Christians, this means returning to Scripture, especially the Gospels. It means seeing Jesus within his Jewish world rather than forcing him into modern categories. It means paying attention to what made the first believers willing to suffer and die. It means listening to Christians from other cultures who see what we may have overlooked. It means allowing Jesus to challenge us instead of simply affirm us.

This kind of restoration will not be easy. We may discover that some images of Jesus we cherish are incomplete or distorted. Still, the work is worth it. A Jesus conformed to our preferences cannot save us. Only the real Messiah—the one who confronts our assumptions, demands our allegiance, and offers true life—is worth following.

READ AND RESPOND

Read 2 Timothy 3:14-17; Hebrews 13:8; Revelation 1:12-18.

1. Paul tells Timothy that Scripture equips God's people. How does regular engagement with Scripture help us recognize the real Jesus instead of a culturally shaped version? What role does Scripture currently play in helping you discern who Jesus is?

2. Hebrews tells us Jesus Christ is the same yesterday, today, and forever. How does Jesus' unchanging nature challenge the ways we've adjusted him to fit our preferences or our culture?

3. Take a moment to reflect on these questions:

   - Does my picture of Jesus challenge my culture or mostly affirm it?
   - Do I read Scripture in ways that allow Jesus to confront my assumptions?
   - Do I learn from Christians in other cultures who see Jesus differently than I do?
   - Am I willing to follow Jesus as he truly is, not just as I want him to be?

   Which one of these questions stands out most to you right now—and why?

4. In Revelation, Jesus appears with blazing eyes, a thunderous voice, and overwhelming glory. Even John falls at his feet in awe. How does this picture of Jesus stretch or disrupt your usual image of him?

5. How would you explain what it means to follow a Jesus who inspires both closeness and holy fear?

6. What is one concrete step you will take this week to recover a clearer picture of the real Messiah? (For example: reading one of the Gospels with fresh attention, listening to a believer from another culture, or asking God to reveal how your view of Jesus has been shaped more by preference than truth.) Write down your step and commit to it.

DAY 5

WRAP-UP

Use this time to go back and complete any of the study and reflection questions from previous days that you were unable to finish. Make a note of any revelations you've had and reflect on any growth or personal insights you've gained.

Read chapter 6 in *The Missing Messiah* before the next group session. Use the space provided to make note of anything in that chapter that challenges you or encourages you.

SESSION 3

DISCOVERING THE MESSIAH

SESSION 3

GROUP STUDY

WELCOME

A Bedouin shepherd boy was searching for a lost goat near the Dead Sea. He tossed a rock into a cave and heard pottery shatter. Curious, he climbed inside. What he discovered would reshape biblical scholarship: ancient scrolls sealed in clay jars, untouched for nearly two thousand years.

These writings became known as the Dead Sea Scrolls. They included copies of almost every Old Testament book, among them a complete scroll of Isaiah dated to around 125 BC—more than a thousand years older than any manuscript scholars had previously encountered.

When experts compared that Isaiah scroll with much later copies, they were stunned. Despite centuries of hand copying separating them, the texts were nearly identical. The passages Christians identify as messianic—the Suffering Servant, the promised child, the coming King—were clearly present long before the time of Jesus.[1]

These prophecies were not written after the fact to match his life. They already existed. They had been preserved, studied, and debated for generations.

The scrolls confirmed what Christians had always believed: that the prophets spoke about the Messiah with clarity and detail. They described his birthplace, his mission, his suffering, and his reign. These weren't vague predictions that could be morphed to fit anyone. They were specific enough that when Jesus appeared, those who knew the Scriptures recognized what was happening.

This matters. You can't invent a messiah and then rewrite ancient texts to support him. The Scriptures were already public, guarded by communities spread across time and geography. When Jesus arrived, the question was not whether the prophecies existed; the question was whether this carpenter from Nazareth truly fulfilled them.

The early church answered yes. The Gospel writers consistently pointed back to the prophets—not to create a story but to recognize one. They believed that the promises had been waiting and that Jesus stepped directly into them.

This week, we will listen again to those prophetic promises in their original setting. We will see that the Messiah was not a mystery to be solved but a promise to be kept. The prophets told us who to watch for. The question is whether we are still looking at that Messiah—or whether we've settled for another.

CONNECT

What from this week's reading stood out to you, or what did you especially need to hear?

Have you ever had an experience when something you waited for or prepared for turned out differently than you expected? How did you respond?

WATCH

Watch the session 3 video together. *To access this video session, follow the instructions located at the front of this book.*

NOTES

DISCUSS

Discuss what you read this week and what you learned from the video by working through the following questions:

1. Invite someone to read Isaiah 53:3-6. This passage describes a Messiah who suffers for others rather than conquering by force. How does this challenge the expectation of a powerful military Messiah? Why do you think God's people needed a Savior who would suffer before he would reign?

2. The book discusses how the Messiah was predicted to be a prophet like Moses, a priest like Melchizedek, and a king like David—all three offices in one person. Why is it significant that no one in Israel's history ever held all three roles simultaneously? What does this tell us about the uniqueness of Jesus?

3. Invite someone to read Micah 5:2. This prophecy names Bethlehem as the birthplace of Israel's future ruler—something the infant Jesus would not have had control over. Why does the specificity of prophecies like this matter? How does it strengthen the case that Jesus is the promised Messiah?

4. Chapter 6 in the book describes how Jesus fulfilled prophecies about his lineage, birthplace, ministry, suffering, death, and resurrection. Which type of prophecy do you find most compelling as evidence that Jesus is the Messiah? Why does that particular fulfillment stand out to you?

5. Many people in Jesus' day knew the Scriptures but missed the Messiah because Jesus didn't meet their own expectations. What warning does that give us about letting our expectations override what Scripture says? What expectations do we have that Jesus doesn't meet?

RESPOND

We've explored how the Old Testament prophets predicted the Messiah with remarkable specificity. Take a few minutes to reflect on what it means that God announced his plan centuries in advance and then faithfully fulfilled it.

> You search the Scriptures because you think they give you eternal life. But the Scriptures point to me! Yet you refuse to come to me to receive this life.
>
> **JOHN 5:39-40, NLT**

Jesus told religious experts that the Scriptures—the Old Testament—pointed to him, yet they refused to come to him for life. It's possible to know Scripture and still miss Jesus. How can you avoid studying the

Bible in a way that increases knowledge without leading to a deeper relationship with the Messiah?

The prophets painted a picture of the Messiah across centuries of Scripture. Knowing that God was faithful to fulfill his ancient promises, what current promise of God do you need to trust him for? What will you do this week to demonstrate that trust?

PRAY

Close your time in prayer.

- Thank God for his faithfulness in fulfilling every prophecy about the Messiah.
- Praise him for leaving detailed clues throughout Scripture so we could recognize Jesus when he came.
- Ask the Holy Spirit to help you read the Old Testament with fresh eyes, seeing how it points to Christ.
- Pray for those who, like the religious leaders of Jesus' day, know Scripture but haven't recognized Jesus as Messiah.
- Ask God to give you wisdom to trust his promises even when fulfillment takes longer than you'd prefer, knowing that he always keeps his word.

SESSION 3

PERSONAL STUDY

Throughout this week, we'll examine the prophetic promises that pointed to the Messiah centuries before Jesus was born. Each day will help you see how God wove messianic expectations throughout Israel's history, creating a portrait that Jesus perfectly fulfilled. This week focuses on Scripture—returning to the prophets and promises that anchor our understanding of the Messiah in God's revealed Word rather than human expectations.

As you work through these exercises, write down your responses. (If you're engaging in this study as part of a group, you'll have a few minutes to share your insights at the start of the next session.)

DAY 1

THE PROMISE KEEPER

On June 5, 1944, Dwight D. Eisenhower wrote two letters. One announced the successful invasion of Normandy. The other wasn't meant to be seen unless things went wrong. He kept it in his pocket throughout D-Day. In it, Eisenhower took full responsibility for failure. "If any blame or fault attaches to the attempt," he wrote, "it is mine alone." He was prepared for either outcome, determined to keep his promise to help liberate Europe, even if it cost him everything.[2]

Stories of that kind of resolve stay with us. History remembers leaders who are willing to stand behind their promises. Still, even the strongest human promises have limits. Circumstances change. Plans fail. People die. Eisenhower could commit to responsibility, but he couldn't guarantee victory.

God's promises are different.

When God speaks into history, he doesn't prepare for failure. He doesn't adjust his plans as events unfold. From the moment sin entered the world, God began promising a deliverer—and he kept those promises across centuries and generations. The Messiah was not a backup plan. He was part of the story from the beginning.

The scope is staggering. God promised Abraham that his chosen descendant would bless all nations (see Genesis 22:18). He promised David an heir whose Kingdom would never end (see 2 Samuel 7:12-13). He promised through Isaiah that a virgin would bear a son named Immanuel (see 7:14). Through Micah, he promised that this ruler would come from Bethlehem (see 5:2). Through Zechariah, he promised a King who would arrive humbly, riding on a donkey (see 9:9). Over time, the portrait grew clearer—lineage, birthplace, mission, suffering, resurrection. Different prophets. Different centuries. One unfolding promise.

Then Jesus came: Born in Bethlehem to a virgin. Descended from Abraham and David. Entering Jerusalem on a donkey. Giving his life for sin. Rising from the dead. Every promise was fulfilled—not loosely, not symbolically, but precisely. What no human could orchestrate, God accomplished without fail.

This is more than history. It's hope.

If God kept his promises about the Messiah's first coming, we can trust his promises about the second. If he fulfilled what he spoke about Jesus' birth, death, and resurrection, we can trust what he promises about our resurrection, the completion of his Kingdom, and our future with him. The prophecies about Jesus do more than point to who he is. They reveal who God is: a promise keeper, faithful to the end.

READ AND RESPOND

Read Genesis 12:1-3; 2 Samuel 7:12-16; Genesis 3:15.

1. In Genesis 12, God promises Abraham that through his offspring, all nations of the earth will be blessed. How does this promise shape the way we understand the Messiah's mission? How does it impact the way you live your life?

2. In 2 Samuel 7, God promises David that his throne will be established forever. Why is it significant that the Messiah came from David's line? How does this promise help us see Jesus not just as a spiritual figure but as a rightful King?

3. As you look at the diagram, what do you notice about how God kept pointing his people toward Jesus?

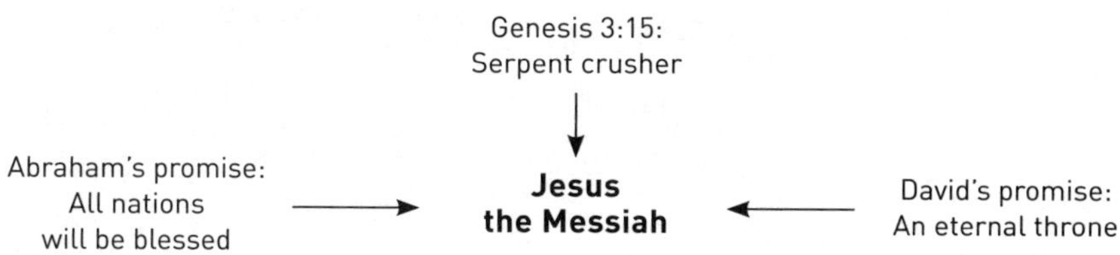

How does seeing this bigger story guard against reducing Jesus to a role we prefer rather than receiving him as the promised Messiah?

4. Chapter 6 of the book explains that Jesus didn't just fulfill one promise but brought together multiple strands of expectation—offspring of Abraham, son of David, Suffering Servant, reigning King. The fulfillment of these promises took a *long* time. In what areas of your life are you tempted to want quick fulfillment rather than trusting God and waiting on him?

5. Chapter 6 shows how Jesus fulfilled promises spanning from Genesis to the prophets. How does it change the way you read the Old Testament when you see the Bible as one unified story pointing to Christ?

DAY 2

THE SUFFERING SERVANT

On January 15, 1944, the German gestapo surrounded a Catholic boys' school in Avon, France. They targeted Father Jacques de Jésus, a Carmelite priest who had enrolled three Jewish children in the school under false names. He had also sheltered a fourth Jewish boy as a worker and employed a Jewish botanist on his staff.

When the gestapo confronted him, Father Jacques refused to acknowledge their authority. "I know only one law: that of the Gospel and Charity," he said.[3] As he was led away with three of the boys, he turned to the students and called out, "Au revoir et à bientôt" ("Goodbye and see you soon").[4] One boy began applauding. Soon the entire school joined in, despite the gestapo's commands for silence.

The three Jewish students and the botanist's family were deported to Auschwitz and murdered. Father Jacques was sent to several concentration camps before reaching Mauthausen. He lived to see liberation in May 1945 but died shortly afterward from the effects of torture and starvation. Freedom arrived too late to save his life.[5]

Father Jacques understood something most people never grasp: Real love doesn't seek safety or self-preservation; it gives itself away. It doesn't cling to power; it releases control for the sake of others. This way of life appears foolish to the world, yet it was prophesied as the way of the Messiah centuries before Jesus was born.

Isaiah 53 portrays a servant who is despised and rejected, familiar with grief and suffering. He carries the pain of others. He is pierced and crushed because of human sin. He goes to death willingly so that many may be made righteous. The servant suffers so others may be saved.

This vision shocked Israel's expectations. They longed for a conquering Messiah, not a suffering one. They anticipated triumph, not execution. They imagined a throne, not a cross. Yet Isaiah foretold a deliverer who would save through sacrifice rather than force.

Centuries later, an Ethiopian official read this passage and asked Philip, "Who is the prophet talking about?" (Acts 8:34). Philip began there and proclaimed Jesus to this man. The Suffering Servant was the Messiah, Jesus, who bore sin, endured injustice, and gave his life so others could live.

This truth reshapes what it means to follow him. If the Messiah came to serve rather than be served, then his people can't chase status or cling to privilege. We don't climb over others to gain advantage. We lay down our lives so others may rise. We release our rights for the good of our neighbors. We refuse revenge and choose forgiveness.

The Suffering Servant calls us to become servants too, willing to bear the cost so that others may find life.

READ AND RESPOND

Read Isaiah 53:1-12; Acts 8:26-35; 1 Peter 2:21-25.

1. Isaiah 53 was written centuries before Jesus, yet it describes precisely what he experienced: suffering, rejection, piercing, silence before accusers, and death among the wicked. When you read this chapter, what details feel especially specific or striking in light of Jesus' life and death?

2. In the chart, you'll see a few of Isaiah's prophecies about the Messiah. Review the accounts of Jesus' trials, death, and burial in the Gospels and record how Jesus fulfilled each one:

Isaiah's Prophecy	How Jesus Fulfilled It
1. Wounded for our transgressions	
2. Despised and rejected	
3. Stood silent before his accusers	
4. Died with the wicked	
5. Buried with the rich	

3. In Acts 8, when Philip meets the Ethiopian official, he begins with Isaiah 53 to explain who Jesus is. Why do you think Philip started there—with Jesus' suffering and death—rather than with his teachings or miracles?

4. Peter says that Christ suffered for us and left an example for us to follow. How does seeing Jesus as the Suffering Servant shape the way you understand suffering in your own life? What would it look like for you to follow his example?

5. Jesus said that the Son of Man came not to be served but to serve and to give his life as a ransom (see Mark 10:45). Where is God inviting you to choose service over self-protection this week? Name one relationship or situation in which you can follow the pattern of the Suffering Servant in a concrete way.

DAY 3

DETAILS ONLY GOD COULD ARRANGE

Mathematician Peter Stoner published a book in 1958 titled *Science Speaks*. In it, he calculated the odds of one person fulfilling just eight messianic prophecies. His estimate was staggering: one chance in 10^{17}—one in 100,000,000,000,000,000. To help readers grasp the scale, Stoner offered an illustration. Imagine the state of Texas covered two feet deep in silver dollars, with one coin marked. The odds of a blindfolded person randomly selecting that coin would be the same as someone accidentally fulfilling those eight prophecies.[6]

Jesus did not fulfill just eight prophecies. He fulfilled *dozens*.

These prophecies include details about his lineage, birthplace, manner of birth, ministry, teaching, entry into Jerusalem, betrayal, death, and resurrection. Many of these were outside his control. As an infant, Jesus didn't choose where he was born, who his ancestors were, or how he would be executed. Yet every detail aligned.

The prophecies themselves are remarkably specific. Micah names Bethlehem in Judah as the Messiah's birthplace. Zechariah describes a King entering Jerusalem on a donkey. The Psalms speak of pierced hands and feet and soldiers casting lots for clothing. Isaiah foretells the Messiah being buried with the rich. These are not vague predictions that could fit anyone. They converge in only one life.

Some critics suggest Jesus or his followers staged events to fit the prophecies. But how would he arrange his own birthplace or ancestry? How would he control Roman execution practices or a soldier's decision to gamble for his clothes? How would he ensure that a wealthy stranger offered his tomb? These details were shaped by forces only God could control.

The prophecies function as God's signature on Jesus' identity. They authenticate the Messiah in ways that can't be manufactured. When prophecy after prophecy finds fulfillment in Jesus, it points to a mission rooted in divine purpose, not human planning.

When we confess Jesus as the Messiah, we aren't inventing a claim. We're recognizing what God declared long ago and confirmed with precision. The prophecies are God's way of saying, "This is the one I sent. Pay attention."

READ AND RESPOND

Read Micah 5:2; Zechariah 9:9; Psalm 22:16-18.

1. Micah predicted that the Messiah would come from the small town of Bethlehem. Why does the specificity of this prophecy matter when considering Jesus' identity?

2. Jesus' intentional choice to ride a donkey was an act of humble obedience to fulfill prophecy, even though it went against worldly expectations of power (see Matthew 21:1-11). What's one way you could choose humility this week, even if it means looking weak or foolish to others?

3. Psalm 22 describes the piercing of hands and feet, public humiliation, and soldiers dividing clothing—long before crucifixion existed. How does a prophecy like this shape your confidence that Jesus' crucifixion was part of God's plan, not a tragic accident?

4. Through the prophecies about the Messiah, God made promises that he fulfilled after a long time. Plot on the graph how your trust tends to rise or fall while you're waiting for God to act.

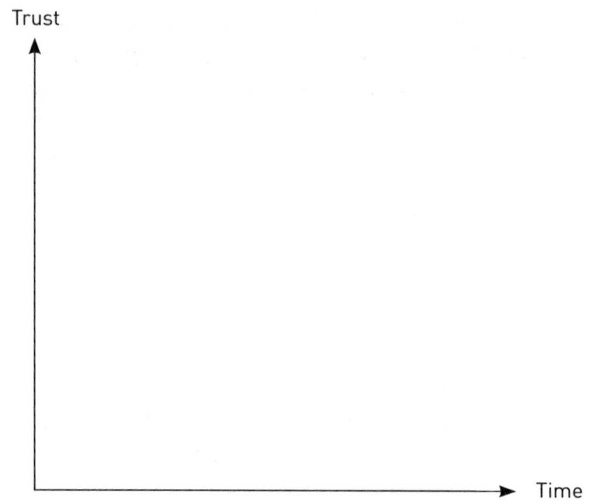

What pattern do you notice about your trust during seasons of waiting?

5. The fulfillment of these detailed prophecies demonstrates God's faithfulness over centuries. If God was precise and trustworthy in keeping these promises, what is something you can trust him with right now? What's one step you can take this week that reflects that trust?

DAY 4

WHEN PROPHECY MET HISTORY

David Ben-Gurion stood in a Tel Aviv museum and read Israel's declaration of independence. It was May 14, 1948, and after nearly two thousand years of exile, the Jewish people finally had a nation again. What had seemed impossible—for a scattered, persecuted people with no homeland—had become reality, just as prophets like Ezekiel and Isaiah had foretold centuries earlier.

When prophecy intersects with history, abstract promises become concrete realities. Ancient words take on flesh and time. What once sounded impossible becomes undeniable.

This is what happened with Jesus.

For centuries, Israel carried promises about a coming Messiah. Then, at a specific moment in history—under Roman rule, during the reign of Caesar Augustus and the governorship of Herod the Great—the waiting ended. Prophecy and history collided. The Messiah came.

The Gospel writers were intent on showing this convergence. Matthew, writing to Jewish readers, points out how events "fulfilled what was spoken through the prophet" (Matthew 13:35). Luke, the careful historian, anchors events in time—under that governor, in the fifteenth year of this ruler, Caesar (see Luke 3:1). Their message is clear: These are not myths but events that happened in real places at real moments in history.

This historical context sets Christianity apart. Many religions rest on timeless ideas or legendary figures; Christianity stakes everything on a person who lived in history and fulfilled specific prophecies. If those prophecies were to fail, the faith would collapse. The early Christians knew this. They weren't offering spiritual symbolism; they were declaring that God had acted in history through Jesus, exactly as promised.

That grounding matters. Faith is not a leap away from history but a step toward it. The Messiah is not an idea but a person—one who taught, healed, suffered, died under Roman authority, and rose from the grave. Witnesses saw him. Prophecies converged in him. Heaven and history met in Jesus.

When we confess Jesus as the Messiah, we are making a historical claim. Look at the promises. Look at the record. Look at how predictions and fulfillment converged in one life. This was not coincidence or manipulation—it was divine orchestration. God spoke through the prophets, acted through Jesus, and changed the course of the world.

READ AND RESPOND

Read Luke 3:1-2; Galatians 4:4-5; Matthew 1:22-23; 2:5-6.

1. Luke carefully anchors John the Baptist's ministry in real, historical figures and dates. Why does it matter that Christianity is rooted in verifiable history rather than presented as merely a spiritual or symbolic story?

2. In Galatians 4, Paul says Jesus came "when the set time had fully come," exactly when God intended (verse 4). How does the idea of God's perfect timing speak to you when you're waiting for something in your own life?

3. Draw a large circle and divide it into four sections, like a pie chart. Write a label for each section: "Roman roads and peace," "Greek language widespread," "Jewish diaspora," and "Prophetic expectation at peak." In each section, write one way this factor helped the gospel spread quickly in the early church.

How does this visual show how the Messiah appeared "when the set time had fully come"?

4. Matthew connects Jesus' birth and early life to multiple prophecies to show that he is the Messiah. When doubts about Jesus arise in your own mind or when questions come up in conversations with others, do you find yourself going back to the evidence or relying on something else? What would strengthen your confidence?

5. Christianity is grounded in specific historical claims: places, rulers, events, and eyewitnesses. How does knowing the historical roots of Christianity shape the way you talk about your faith? What's one way you can grow more confident in presenting Christianity as both historically credible and spiritually meaningful?

DAY 5

WRAP-UP

Use this time to go back and complete any of the study and reflection questions from previous days that you were unable to finish. Make a note of any revelations you've had and reflect on any growth or personal insights you've gained.

Read chapters 7–8 in *The Missing Messiah* before the next group session. Use the space provided to make note of anything in those chapters that stands out to you or encourages you.

SESSION 4

THE MESSIAH NO ONE SAW COMING

SESSION 4

GROUP STUDY

WELCOME

Steve Jobs stepped onto a stage with something hidden behind his back. The crowd at Macworld leaned in. Apple had been teasing a major announcement for weeks. Reporters expected a better laptop. Some guessed a tablet. Others imagined a phone with email. Jobs smiled and revealed something no one had fully anticipated: a slim device that combined phone, Internet, music, and camera in one.

The iPhone was not just an improvement; it redefined what a phone could be.

The audience knew immediately this was different. Jobs wasn't offering a better flip phone. He was placing a small computer in their pocket. Expectations weren't met; they were surpassed. Within a few years, smartphones would reshape how people communicated, worked, and lived.

There are some parallels with what happened when Jesus came.

Israel had been waiting for the Messiah for generations. Their expectations were shaped by both Scripture and their experiences.

They assumed the Messiah would be a king like David, a leader who would defeat their enemies and restore their national strength. They were looking for a stronger version of what they already knew—a familiar solution to a painful problem.

Jesus disrupted that vision.

He was not an upgraded version of Israel's past. He was something altogether new. He fulfilled the roles of Adam, Abraham, Moses, and David, yet he also exceeded them all. He wasn't just king, prophet, or priest; he embodied all three. He didn't simply improve Israel's story; he brought it to completion and opened it to the world.

Since Jesus went beyond expectations, many religious leaders missed him. They wanted a Messiah who fit their categories and worked within their system. Jesus challenged the system itself. He welcomed the excluded, ate with sinners, healed when he was told not to, and claimed an authority that belonged to God alone.

This week, we'll explore how Jesus exceeded expectations and revealed himself as more than Israel imagined. He redefined what the Messiah was meant to be.

The real question is not whether Jesus meets expectations; it's whether we're willing to let him exceed ours.

CONNECT

Share one insight or challenge from your personal studies this week. What stood out to you most?

Have you ever received something that far exceeded what you expected? What was it, and how did you respond?

WATCH

Watch the session 4 video together. *To access this video session, follow the instructions located at the front of this book.*

NOTES

DISCUSS

1. Invite someone to read Romans 5:12-19. Paul contrasts Adam, who brought sin and death, with Jesus, who brings grace and life. How does seeing Jesus as the "new Adam" shape your understanding of what he came to undo and restore?

2. Chapter 7 in *The Missing Messiah* explains that Jesus is greater than Moses—not repeating Moses' work but completing it. For instance:

   - Moses gave the law, but Jesus fulfills it.
   - Moses led Israel out of slavery, but Jesus frees us from sin itself.
   - Moses never entered the Promised Land, but Jesus opens the way to eternal life.

   Why is it significant that Jesus doesn't just improve on what Moses did but brings it to fulfillment? What does that reveal about who Jesus is?

3. Invite someone to read Hebrews 1:1-4. We're told that God spoke through prophets in the past but has now spoken through his Son, who is the exact representation of God. Jesus is the final and ultimate Word from God. How does this passage challenge the tendency to see Jesus as simply a great teacher or prophet?

4. Jesus was both fully human and fully divine. Why does that matter? What would be missing if he were only one or the other?

5. Many first-century Jews expected a political and military Messiah, but Jesus came preaching humility, sacrifice, and a different kind of Kingdom. How do Jesus' priorities challenge what we naturally expect or want him to do today?

RESPOND

We've explored how Jesus exceeded expectations by fulfilling and surpassing every major figure in Israel's history. Take a few minutes to reflect on how your expectations of Jesus might be too small.

> All glory to God, who is able, through his mighty power at work within us, to accomplish infinitely more than we might ask or think. Glory to him in the church and in Christ Jesus through all generations forever and ever! Amen.
>
> **EPHESIANS 3:20-21, NLT**

Paul says God is able to do far more than we ask or imagine through his power at work in us. Where might you be limiting Jesus to what feels reasonable or familiar instead of trusting him to work beyond your expectations?

Jesus often exceeded and disrupted people's expectations rather than fulfilling them. What's one area of your life where you sense Jesus inviting you to release your expectations and trust who he really is? What's one specific step you can take in response this week?

PRAY

Close your time by praying.

- Praise God for sending a Messiah who exceeded all expectations—a Messiah who is greater than any other king, prophet, or priest.
- Thank Jesus for being the new Adam who fixes what was broken, the true Israel who fulfills what the nation couldn't, and the Son of God who reveals the Father perfectly.
- Ask the Holy Spirit to expand your vision of who Jesus is, to challenge expectations that are too small, and to help you embrace the true Jesus, who is infinitely more than you've imagined.
- Pray for humility to admit when you've tried to domesticate Jesus by trying to fit him into your preferences rather than worshiping him as he truly is.

SESSION 4

PERSONAL STUDY

Throughout this week, we'll explore how Jesus surpassed every expectation and exceeded every comparison. Each day will help you see how Jesus didn't just fulfill what the prophets predicted but went infinitely beyond it, revealing himself as both fully human and fully divine. This week focuses on expectations—how Jesus fulfilled God's promises while simultaneously shattering the expectations people had of him.

As you work through these exercises, write down your responses. (If you're engaging in this study as part of a group, you'll have a few minutes to share your insights at the start of the next session.)

DAY 1

GREATER THAN ADAM

Picture a master violinist preparing for a concert. She tunes the instrument, adjusts the bridge, tests the bow. Everything is carefully calibrated. She begins to play . . . and something goes wrong. A string snaps. The music stops. The instrument cannot fulfill its purpose because one crucial component has failed.

This is humanity's story.

God created humans with care, forming them in his image and designing them to reflect his glory in harmony with him. Everything was tuned for life as it was meant to be. Then a critical string—human obedience—snapped. Adam and Eve chose rebellion over trust. Sin entered the world, and death followed. Creation itself went out of tune.

This led to the inevitable question: Could the instrument be restored, or was the damage final? Some believe we can fix ourselves through effort and discipline. Others conclude we are beyond repair. Christianity declares something different. God sent a second Adam to succeed where the first failed. Jesus came as the true human—the one who would bring creation back into alignment with God and with the rest of the created order.

Paul explains this in Romans 5: Through Adam came sin and death. Through Jesus came righteousness and life. Adam was tested in a garden and failed. Jesus was tested in the wilderness and prevailed. Adam reached for equality with God. Jesus humbled himself. Adam's disobedience spread death. Jesus' obedience opens the way to life.

Jesus is what Adam was meant to be—and far more. Adam bore God's image. Jesus is the perfect image of God and is God himself. Adam received authority over creation. Jesus holds authority over creation, redemption, and resurrection. Adam introduced death. Jesus defeated it. Jesus doesn't merely repair what was broken; he elevates humanity beyond Eden to something greater.

This means that union with Christ is more than forgiveness—it's transformation. The broken string isn't just replaced; the instrument is remade. In Christ, we become new creations (see 2 Corinthians 5:17). We're adopted into God's family, filled with his Spirit, and promised resurrection life. Jesus doesn't return us to Adam's beginning; he leads us to a future Adam never reached—a future marked by full and lasting union with God.

READ AND RESPOND

Read Romans 5:12-21; 1 Corinthians 15:20-22, 45-49; Philippians 2:5-11.

1. In Romans 5, Paul contrasts Adam's failure with Christ's obedience and says that where sin increased, grace increased even more. How does seeing Jesus as the second Adam give you hope that grace can reach deeper than the effects of sin in your own life?

2. In 1 Corinthians 15, Paul says the first Adam became a living being but the last Adam became a life-giving spirit who comes from heaven. How does this passage challenge the idea that Jesus was merely a good moral teacher? What do you think it means that Jesus doesn't just model life but actually gives life?

3. Compare Adam and Jesus:

Adam	Jesus (the second Adam)
Tested in a garden → failed	Tested in a wilderness → prevailed
Reached for what was forbidden → brought sin	Refused temptation → brought righteousness
Disobeyed God's command → brought condemnation	Obeyed the Father fully → brought justification
Brought death to humanity	Brings life to humanity
Hid from God after sinning	Moved toward God in trust and obedience

Which of these contrasts are you most grateful for? Which do you need to embrace?

4. Philippians 2 shows that Jesus humbled himself, obeyed the Father, and accepted death on a cross, while Adam grasped for being like God and brought death. How does Jesus' humility reveal a different view of power and greatness than Adam had? What does this teach us about what true greatness looks like in God's Kingdom?

5. Because Jesus is the second Adam, those who belong to him are made new—not repaired but transformed. Where do you most need to experience that transforming power right now?

6. What is one concrete way you can live as a new creation rather than slipping back into old, Adam-like patterns?

DAY 2

GREATER THAN MOSES

Every culture has a founding figure—someone whose influence shapes everything that comes after. George Washington helped define American democracy. Confucius shaped Chinese thought. Muhammad established the pillars of Islam. Their words become authoritative. Their lives become patterns. Their legacies become the lenses through which their followers see the world.

For Israel, that figure was Moses. He was not only a leader but the lawgiver who met God face-to-face, the deliverer who led Israel out of slavery, and the mediator who stood between God and the people. His teaching shaped every part of an Israelite's life. To be Jewish was to live under the Torah Moses received.

That's why the Gospel writers' claims about Jesus were so shocking. They were not merely saying Jesus mattered; they were saying he surpassed the founding figure of Judaism. Moses gave the law; Jesus fulfills it. Moses led Israel through the sea; Jesus leads people through death into life. Moses provided manna; Jesus offers himself as the bread of life. Moses brought water from a rock; Jesus gives living water. Moses lifted up a bronze serpent for healing; Jesus was lifted up on a cross for salvation.

The comparison becomes explicit in Hebrews. Moses was a servant in God's house; Jesus is the Son over God's house. Moses served within what God was building; Jesus is the heir. Moses pointed toward rest; Jesus *is* that rest. Moses mediated the old covenant; Jesus established the new covenant through his own blood. Moses reflected God's glory for a moment; Jesus reveals God's glory without fading.

This doesn't diminish Moses, but even Moses knew he was not the final word. He promised that God would raise up another prophet like him (see Deuteronomy 18:15-18). Moses understood that his role was to prepare the way.

Jesus is the one Moses anticipated. He is the deliverer Moses foreshadowed and the mediator Moses represented. But Jesus does what Moses could not. He frees people not only from oppression but from sin. He writes God's law not on stone but on human hearts. He offers not temporary forgiveness but lasting redemption through his own sacrifice. Jesus is greater than Moses because he completes the mission Moses could only begin.

READ AND RESPOND

Read Hebrews 3:1-6; John 1:14-18; Matthew 5:17-20.

1. Hebrews 3 contrasts Moses and Jesus: Moses was faithful as a servant in God's house, but Jesus is faithful as the Son over God's house. What does this difference between servant and Son tell you about Jesus' authority? How does approaching Jesus as the Son change the way you relate to him compared to how people in the Old Testament related to Moses?

2. John says the law came through Moses but grace and truth come through Jesus. Moses encountered God's glory, yet Jesus fully reveals God. How does Jesus make God known in ways Moses could not?

3. Reflect on how Moses pointed to Jesus:

Moses	Jesus
Led Israel out of slavery	Frees people from slavery to sin
Led the people through the Red Sea	Leads people through death into new life
Provided manna in the wilderness	Is the true bread from heaven
Lifted up the bronze serpent for healing	Was lifted up on the cross for healing and salvation
Delivered God's law to the people	Fulfills the law and writes it on hearts

How does this help you to see the entire Bible as one unified story about Jesus?

4. In Matthew 5:17-20, Jesus says he came not to abolish the law but to fulfill it. What did Jesus mean by this claim? Why do you think God didn't send him to enforce the law?

5. Moses led the people toward the Promised Land but never entered it himself. Jesus not only enters God's promised rest but opens the way for others to enter with him. In what ways are you tempted to rely on your own effort or performance instead of trusting what Jesus has already accomplished? What's one specific way you can rest more fully in Christ's finished work this week?

DAY 3

GREATER THAN DAVID

A shepherd boy once stood before a giant with only a sling and a few stones. Everyone else saw an impossible fight. He saw an infinite God. The stone flew, and the giant fell. And Israel found its greatest king.

David became the standard by which all future kings were measured. He was a man after God's own heart, a warrior who won battles, and a poet who wrote psalms. God promised that David's throne would endure, that one of his descendants would reign forever. From that point on, Israel's hope for the Messiah was shaped by David. They longed for a king who would restore his glory.

Yet David was far from ideal. He committed adultery and arranged a murder to hide his sin. His family was marked by violence, betrayal, and rebellion. His victories brought success but also great bloodshed. Though he longed to build God's Temple, he wasn't allowed to do so. David pointed toward the perfect king, but he couldn't be that king himself.

Jesus was born in David's hometown and descended from his lineage. But where David fought physical enemies, Jesus defeated spiritual foes and the sin and death they wrought. Where David's kingdom was limited, Jesus' Kingdom extends to every nation. Where David's reign ended, Jesus' reign is eternal. Where David failed, Jesus lived with perfect faithfulness. Where David wielded a sword, Jesus carried a cross.

Jesus highlighted this difference with a question: If the Messiah is David's son, why does David call him Lord? The answer? The Messiah would come from David yet stand far above him. Jesus wasn't merely part of David's legacy; he was the King that David served (see Luke 20:41-44).

That means Jesus' Kingdom is unlike any earthly kingdom. It doesn't rise and fall. It's the everlasting Kingdom foretold by Daniel—one marked by righteousness, peace, and unending rule (see Daniel 2:44; 7:14).

READ AND RESPOND

Read 2 Samuel 7:8-16; Matthew 22:41-46; Luke 1:30-33.

1. God promised David that his kingdom would endure forever, even though many of his descendants failed as kings. What does God's faithfulness to this promise teach you about how he keeps his word, even when people fall short?

2. In Matthew 22, Jesus asks the Pharisees how the Messiah can be both David's son and David's Lord (see Psalm 110:1). What does this exchange reveal about who Jesus is? How can he be both fully human, descended from David, and yet greater than David?

3. King David points forward to Jesus as the one true, eternal King. Consider these contrasts:

David	Jesus
Conquered physical enemies	Conquered sin, death, and Satan
Reigned over Israel only	Reigns over all nations
Established a temporary kingdom	Establishes an eternal Kingdom
Failed morally and needed forgiveness	Lived without sin and brings forgiveness
Ruled by the sword	Rules through sacrificial love

How do these contrasts help you understand why Jesus is the greater King? Which contrast most challenges you to live differently?

4. How does Jesus' kind of kingship—one that began in a manger and was established through a cross—challenge what you typically look for in leaders or what you hope a "kingdom" will provide?

5. In Luke 1:32-33, the angel says that Jesus is an eternal King with an eternal Kingdom. In what areas of your life are you tempted to put your hope in political solutions, strong leaders, or earthly systems to fix things? How can remembering that Jesus is the forever King shift where you place your ultimate trust and hope?

DAY 4

THE GOD-MAN

C. S. Lewis argued that Jesus leaves us with limited options. He was either a liar who knowingly deceived people, a lunatic who believed he was God when he was not, or exactly who he claimed to be—the Lord. What we cannot do, Lewis said, is reduce Jesus to merely a good moral teacher. People who are good teachers don't claim to forgive sins, receive worship, or speak as God.[1]

The early church spent centuries wrestling with what Jesus claimed about himself. They came to affirm a mystery at the heart of Christian faith: Jesus is fully God and fully human. Not God pretending to be human. Not a human specially empowered by God. Fully God. Fully human. Two complete natures united in one person. Christians came to call this the incarnation: God taking on flesh without ceasing to be God.

This proved difficult for many. Some denied Jesus' divinity to protect his humanity. Others denied his humanity to preserve his divinity. Confusion followed. In AD 451, the Council of Chalcedon gave the church careful language: Jesus is truly God and truly human, with two natures united without confusion, division, or separation.

Why does this matter? Because salvation requires both. Jesus had to be fully human to represent us, to live faithfully in our place, and to die on our behalf. Only a human can stand in for humanity. But he also had to be fully God. Only God can bear the full weight of everyone's sin, defeat death, and restore creation.

The Messiah no one expected was more than a king, prophet, and priest. He was God entering his own creation, revealing who God truly is and what humanity was meant to be. Fully God, so he could save. Fully human, so he could stand in our place. The God-man is not just a theological idea. He is the only Savior who can truly bring us home.

READ AND RESPOND

Read John 1:1-14; Colossians 1:15-20; 2:9; Hebrews 4:15.

1. John's Gospel opens with stunning claims: "In the beginning was the Word, and the Word was with God, and the Word was God. . . . The Word became flesh and made his dwelling among us" (verses 1, 14). John is declaring that Jesus existed eternally as God and then became human without ceasing to be God. Why is it crucial that Jesus is both eternal God and incarnate human? What would be lost if he were only one or the other?

2. Jesus was fully human and fully God. Add to the list why both were necessary.

Fully Human	Fully God
• To represent humanity	• To offer a sacrifice worthy of saving us
• To live the life we should have lived	• To defeat sin and death with divine power
•	•
•	•
•	•
•	•
•	•

3. In Colossians 1:15-20, Paul describes Jesus as both the Creator of all things and the one who reconciles all things through the cross. How does seeing Jesus as both Creator and our reconciler shape the way you understand what he accomplished through his death?

4. In Colossians 2:9, Paul declares that in Christ "all the fullness of the Deity lives in bodily form." This is one of Scripture's clearest statements that Jesus is fully God in human flesh. The Greek word for "deity" (*theotēs*) means the very nature and essence of God—not just divine attributes but divinity itself.[2] How does this verse answer those who claim that Jesus was just a good man or a great prophet but not God?

5. Because Jesus is fully God and fully human, he understands human weakness (see Hebrews 4:15) and has the power to save completely (see Hebrews 7:25). Where in your life do you need Jesus' compassion for human struggle and his divine power to bring real change? What is one specific burden or struggle you will intentionally bring to him this week?

DAY 5

WRAP-UP

Use this time to go back and complete any of the study and reflection questions from previous days that you were unable to finish. Make a note of any revelations you've had and reflect on any growth or personal insights you've gained.

Read chapter 9 in *The Missing Messiah* before the next group session. Use the space provided to make note of anything in that chapter that stands out to you or encourages you.

SESSION 5

THE COMEBACK THAT PROVED HIS MESSIAHSHIP

SESSION 5

GROUP STUDY

WELCOME

Imagine attending a funeral where the deceased suddenly walks in. Not as a ghost or vision but physically alive, asking what everyone is crying about. The shock would be indescribable. Every assumption about death would instantly shatter.

This is precisely what happened on the first Easter morning.

The resurrection was not a comforting metaphor about Jesus' teachings living on. It was not something mystical experienced by the disciples. It was a historical event that validated every claim Jesus made about being the Messiah. The tomb was empty. The body was gone. And Jesus appeared to more than five hundred witnesses, eating fish, inviting Thomas to touch his wounds, and spending forty days teaching about the Kingdom of God.

Without the resurrection, Christianity collapses. If Jesus had stayed dead, he would be just another failed messianic pretender. His teachings, though beautiful, would carry no more authority than any other moral philosopher. His promises of eternal life would be empty words. As Paul bluntly states, "If Christ has not been raised, your faith is futile; you are still in your sins" (1 Corinthians 15:17).

But the resurrection changed everything.

It proved Jesus was who he claimed to be. It demonstrated God's power over death. It established Jesus as the eternal King who will never die. It guaranteed our own future resurrection. And it marked Jesus' coronation—the moment when the crucified carpenter was publicly declared as Lord of all creation.

The early church didn't just believe Jesus rose from the dead—they staked everything on it. They faced persecution, imprisonment, and death rather than deny that the tomb was empty. Their message was not just "Jesus taught us to be kind." It was "Jesus is alive—he is King! And every knee will bow to him."

This week, we'll explore how the resurrection is the linchpin of Jesus' messiahship. Without it, he is a teacher. With it, he is the eternal King. The question is not just "Do you believe Jesus rose from the dead?" The question is "Will you submit to the authority of the resurrected King?"

His comeback proved his kingship. Our response determines our eternity.

CONNECT

Share one insight or challenge from your personal studies this week. What stood out to you most?

If you could ask Jesus one question about the resurrection, what would it be?

WATCH

Watch the session 5 video together. *To access this video session, follow the instructions located at the front of this book.*

NOTES

DISCUSS

1. Invite someone to read 1 Corinthians 15:14-17. Paul says that without the resurrection, our faith is futile and we are still in our sins. Why is the resurrection essential to Christianity? Why is it more than just a hopeful ending to the Jesus story?

2. Have someone read Acts 2:29-32. Peter, speaking in this passage, connects the resurrection directly to Jesus' enthronement as King, pointing to God's promise to David in Psalm 16. How does viewing the resurrection as Jesus' coronation change how we understand and celebrate Easter?

3. Chapter 9 of *The Missing Messiah* argues that Western individualism has reduced the resurrection to a personal promise of heaven while downplaying its announcement that Jesus reigns as King right now. How have you seen this play out in how Christians talk about the resurrection? What do you think is lost when we think of the resurrection that way?

4. Read Matthew 28:18-20 aloud. After his resurrection, Jesus declares that "all authority in heaven and on earth has been given to me." If Jesus truly has all authority now, not just in the future, what implications does this have for how we live today—in our work, relationships, attitudes, finances, and citizenship?

5. Jesus' resurrection resolved the paradox of how the Messiah could die yet live forever. How does understanding this help us make sense of Jesus as both the Suffering Servant and the eternal King?

RESPOND

In this session, we have seen how the resurrection validates Jesus' kingship and calls us to live under his authority now. Take a few minutes to reflect using the following passage:

> Being found in appearance as a man,
> he humbled himself
> by becoming obedient to death—
> even death on a cross!
>
> Therefore God exalted him to the highest place
> and gave him the name that is above every name,
> that at the name of Jesus every knee should bow,
> in heaven and on earth and under the earth,

> and every tongue acknowledge that Jesus Christ is Lord,
> to the glory of God the Father.
>
> **PHILIPPIANS 2:8–11**

According to these verses, Jesus' humiliation led to his exaltation. How does recognizing that Jesus is now exalted and reigning challenge the areas of your life where you've been living as if his authority is optional?

Paul says that every knee will bow and every tongue will confess that Jesus is Lord. What would it look like for you to "bow the knee" to Jesus in a specific area where you've been resisting his authority?

PRAY

Close your time together in prayer.

- Thank Jesus for conquering death and proving his kingship through the resurrection.
- Confess any areas where you've treated his lordship as optional.
- Ask him to help you live under his authority in every sphere of your life.
- Pray that your group would be witnesses to the resurrected and reigning King.

SESSION 5

PERSONAL STUDY

Throughout this week, we'll examine the resurrection not just as a promise of your own future resurrection but as the event that established Jesus as the reigning King. Each day will help you see how the resurrection is the linchpin of Jesus' messiahship and what it means to live under his authority today. This week focuses on resurrection authority—the moment when God publicly vindicated Jesus as Messiah and King by raising him from the dead.

As you work through each of these exercises, write down your responses to the questions. (If you're engaging in this study as part of a group, you'll have a few minutes to share your insights at the start of the next session.)

DAY 1

THE LINCHPIN OF FAITH

The Tacoma Narrows Bridge opened in July 1940, spanning the Tacoma Narrows strait in Washington state. Engineers admired its sleek design. At the time, it was the third-longest suspension bridge in the world. For four months, it carried traffic without incident.

Then, on November 7, moderate winds caused the bridge to begin swaying. The movement intensified, and witnesses watched in disbelief as the roadway twisted and tore itself apart. Within hours, the entire structure collapsed into the Puget Sound. Engineers later discovered that the bridge lacked sufficient stiffening trusses. Turns out, when a critical structural element is missing, no amount of elegance or innovation can prevent failure.[1]

Paul understood that Christianity has the same kind of structural dependency. Addressing the church in Corinth, he wrote with striking clarity: "If Christ has not been raised, our preaching is useless and so is your faith" (1 Corinthians 15:14).

Paul was not claiming that the resurrection merely strengthens Christian belief. He was saying that without it, there is no Christianity at all. If Jesus didn't rise from the dead, faith collapses under its own weight. Hope becomes wishful thinking. Forgiveness turns into fiction.

Everything Christians claim about Jesus depends on whether he walked out of the tomb.

This conviction explains the courage of the early Christians. They were willing to die not for inspiring moral teachings or a helpful philosophy of life but because they believed they had encountered the risen Christ and could not deny what they had seen. For them, the resurrection changed everything. If it happened, nothing else ultimately mattered. If it didn't, nothing else was worth defending.

The resurrection still demands that same clarity from us. It's not simply a comforting belief or an inspiring symbol. If Jesus rose from the dead, then he is Lord, and his claims on our lives are absolute. If he did not, Christianity is an impressive structure built on a fatal flaw.

The resurrection is not one doctrine among many. It's the essential support that holds our entire faith together.

READ AND RESPOND

Read 1 Corinthians 15:12-22; Romans 10:9.

1. In 1 Corinthians 15, Paul lists several devastating consequences for our faith if Christ has not been raised. Which of these consequences surprises you most? Which of these consequences challenges your understanding of why the resurrection matters?

2. Paul says, "If only for this life we have hope in Christ, we are of all people most to be pitied" (verse 19). Why would Christians be pitiable without Christ's resurrection and without the hope of our own resurrection?

3. Paul calls Jesus "the first of a great harvest of all who have died," meaning his resurrection guarantees ours (verse 20, NLT). How should understanding Jesus' resurrection as the first of many change the way you think about death—both your own and the death of loved ones?

4. In Romans 10, Paul says that salvation requires both confessing Jesus as Lord and believing that God raised him from the dead. Why do you think both confession and belief in the resurrection are essential? What would you say it means to confess Jesus as Lord in light of his resurrection?

5. The first Christians were willing to suffer and even die because they had seen Jesus, risen from the dead. If someone asked you why you believe the resurrection is true, what would you point to first? How could you explain it in a simple, honest way to someone who is skeptical?

DAY 2

THE KING WHO WOULD NEVER DIE

Qin Shi Huang, the first emperor of unified China, was obsessed with achieving immortality. He commissioned alchemists to create elixirs of eternal life. He sent expeditions to find mythical islands where immortals supposedly lived. He consumed mercury-laden compounds, believing they would preserve his life forever. Ironically, these "immortality" treatments likely hastened his death at age forty-nine.

His elaborate tomb—guarded by the famous Terra-Cotta Army—was designed to extend his reign into eternity. But despite his power, his wealth, and his desperate attempts to cheat death, Emperor Qin died, like every other ruler before and after him. His empire didn't even outlast his son.[2]

History is a graveyard of "eternal" kingdoms—Egypt, Babylon, Persia, Greece, Rome. Each empire believed their power would never end. Each was wrong. The Jews understood this better than most. They had watched their own kingdom crumble, seen Jerusalem burn, and lived under the heel of foreign oppressors.

When they read prophecies about an eternal Messiah—a King whose government would have no end—they faced this impossible paradox: How can any human establish a kingdom that lasts forever? Even if the Messiah lived a thousand years, death would eventually come. And when it did, the promise would be broken.

This is why Jesus' crucifixion devastated his disciples. When he died, their hope died with him. "We had hoped that he was the one who was going to redeem Israel," they said (Luke 24:21). Past tense. A dead Messiah was a failed Messiah.

But Easter morning changed everything. Jesus didn't just come back to life like Lazarus, who eventually died again. He rose to a life that death could never touch. "I am the Living One," he declared. "I was dead, and now look, I am alive for ever and ever!" (Revelation 1:18). Not temporarily alive. Forever alive.

The resurrection solved the unsolvable paradox. Jesus fulfilled both requirements: He died (satisfying the prophecies of the Suffering Servant), and he lives forever (satisfying the expectation of an eternal King). Every empire falls. Every kingdom crumbles. Except his.

READ AND RESPOND

Read Psalm 16:8-11; Acts 2:25-32; Luke 24:13-27; Revelation 1:17-18.

1. In Acts 2, Peter quotes Psalm 16, arguing that David was prophesying about the Messiah's resurrection. How does Peter use this Old Testament passage to prove that Jesus is the Messiah?

2. In Luke 24:13-27, Jesus explains to the disciples on the road to Emmaus how the Scriptures pointed to a suffering and rising Messiah. Why do you think the disciples struggled to reconcile a dying Messiah with their expectations, even though the Scriptures spoke of it?

3. Fill in the blanks about the contrast between Good Friday and the resurrection:

FRIDAY The Disciples' Despair	**SATURDAY**	**SUNDAY** The Game Changed
We had hoped that he was the onewho was going to redeem Israel. Luke 24:21		I am the Living One; I was dead, and now look, I am alive for ever and ever! Revelation 1:18
What was lost:		What was restored/guaranteed:

4. Jesus identifies himself as "the Living One" who was dead but is now alive forever (Revelation 1:17-18). How does this self-description address the Jewish expectation that the Messiah would never die?

5. Today's reading contrasts earthly kingdoms that crumble with Christ's eternal Kingdom. What "kingdoms" (careers, relationships, achievements, security) are you tempted to build your life on, even though they won't last? How does Jesus' claim to be alive forever challenge where you're placing your hope?

DAY 3

THE RESURRECTION AS CORONATION

Millions gathered around radios and newly acquired television sets to witness Queen Elizabeth II's coronation at Westminster Abbey. The ceremony, on June 2, 1953, was steeped in ancient tradition: anointing with holy oil, presentation of royal regalia, and the placing of St. Edward's crown on her head.

But here's what many people didn't realize: Elizabeth had already been queen for sixteen months. Her father, King George VI, had died on February 6, 1952. The moment he died, she became queen. The coronation didn't make her queen—it proclaimed what was already true. The crown didn't grant authority; it announced authority that already existed.[3]

The resurrection was Jesus' coronation ceremony.

We often treat Easter like a funeral that ended surprisingly well—death defeated, tragedy averted, hope restored. But the resurrection wasn't just the happy ending to a sad story. It was God's public declaration of what had always been true: Jesus is King.

Peter understood this. On Pentecost, he didn't preach, "Jesus rose so you can go to heaven someday." He proclaimed, "God has raised this Jesus to life. . . . God has made this Jesus, whom you crucified, both Lord and Messiah" (Acts 2:32, 36). The resurrection established Jesus' throne. The empty tomb announced his reign.

This is why the earliest Christian confession wasn't "Jesus died for my sins." It was "Jesus is Lord." In the Roman Empire, that phrase wasn't a religious sentiment—it was treason. It meant that Caesar wasn't ultimate, that Rome wasn't supreme. Every earthly throne was subordinate to Jesus. And confessing that got people killed.

Easter has become domesticated—a personal promise about our future. While that's true, it's incomplete. The resurrection isn't just about our eventual resurrection—it's about Jesus' present reign. He doesn't just offer eternal life someday. He claims total authority right now.

After rising, Jesus declared, "All authority in heaven and on earth has been given to me" (Matthew 28:18). Not *will be* given. *Has been* given. The coronation happened. The crown is on his head. The question isn't whether he will reign; the question is whether we will submit.

READ AND RESPOND

Read Acts 2:32-36; Philippians 2:5-11; Matthew 28:16-20.

1. In Acts 2:32-36, Peter connects the resurrection directly to Jesus being "made both Lord and Messiah." How does this passage challenge the common view that the resurrection is more about our personal salvation than Jesus' kingship?

2. In Philippians 2, Paul describes Jesus' humiliation and exaltation, saying that because of his obedience to death, God exalted him and gave him "the name that is above every name." What does it mean that Jesus was exalted as a result of his death and resurrection?

3. In the space provided, draw a throne. Below the throne, draw a handful of circles. In each of those circles, write a different aspect of your life: family, career, money, relationships, time, dreams, fears, etc. Draw an arrow from the throne to each circle, indicating that Jesus is the ruler of that part of your life.

In which circles (aspects of your life) are you resisting Jesus' authority? Why do you think that is? In which circles do your friends and neighbors clearly see Jesus' lordship in your life?

4. In Matthew 28, Jesus declares that "all authority in heaven and on earth has been given to me" and then commissions his disciples. How should Jesus' claim of total authority shape the way we approach the great commission?

5. We often think of Easter as simply "Jesus came back to life" rather than "Jesus was publicly crowned King." How does thinking of the resurrection as Jesus' coronation—God's announcement that Jesus holds all authority—change the way you think about or celebrate Easter?

DAY 4

LIVING UNDER THE RESURRECTED KING

Dietrich Bonhoeffer was a German pastor and theologian who understood what it meant to live under Christ's authority when it cost everything. When Hitler rose to power, many German Christians compromised, bending their faith to accommodate Nazi ideology. The state church declared loyalty to the führer. Pastors removed Old Testament readings to appease antisemitism.

Bonhoeffer refused. He openly opposed the Nazi regime, helped Jews escape Germany, and joined a plot to assassinate Hitler. He was arrested in 1943 and imprisoned for two years. On April 9, 1945—just weeks before Germany surrendered—he was executed by hanging.[4]

Before his death, Bonhoeffer wrote *The Cost of Discipleship*, contrasting what he called "cheap grace" with "costly grace." Cheap grace, he argued, is forgiveness without repentance, baptism without discipline, communion without confession. It's the grace we bestow on ourselves—a Jesus who makes no demands. Costly grace, on the other hand, is "costly because it costs a man his life, and it is grace because it gives a man the only true life. . . . Above all, it is costly because it cost God the life of his Son."[5]

The resurrection establishes Jesus not just as Savior but as King. Kings don't rule in private. Their authority isn't personal or optional. If Jesus rose from the dead and holds all authority in heaven and earth, then *every* area of our lives—our money, work, relationships, politics, entertainment, sexuality, ambitions—falls under his reign.

For Bonhoeffer, living under the resurrected King meant his faith couldn't remain private. It meant publicly opposing evil even when it cost him his reputation, his freedom, and ultimately his life. He didn't follow a dead philosopher who left inspiring ideas. He followed a risen Lord who defeated death and demanded total allegiance.

The question facing us is the same one Bonhoeffer faced: Will we settle for cheap grace that costs nothing and changes nothing? Or will we embrace costly grace that requires everything but gives us the only true life?

The King is reigning. The question is, Are we living in allegiance?

READ AND RESPOND

Read John 16:25-33; Ephesians 1:18-21; Romans 8:18-25.

1. Jesus told his disciples, "In this world you will have trouble. But take heart! I have overcome the world" (John 16:33). How does this promise shape the way you think about following a King who has already overcome—even when obedience is costly?

2. In Ephesians 1, Paul prays that believers would know God's "incomparably great power for us who believe"—the same power that raised Christ from the dead. How have you experienced resurrection power in your own life? In what ways do you need to trust that power more?

3. Fill in the chart:

Cheap Grace (Grace Without Cost)	**Costly Grace (Grace That Transforms)**
What it costs:	*What it costs:*
• Nothing • No real change required • No discomfort • • •	• Your life • Your comfort • Your control • • •
What it gives:	*What it gives:*
• Feeling of religion • No real transformation • Easy lifestyle • • •	• The only true life • Real transformation • Deep purpose and meaning • • •
Examples from my life: Where have I settled for cheap grace?	*Where Jesus is calling me:* Where can I embrace costly grace?

4. Bonhoeffer's faith shaped his choices, even when they were costly. What is one situation in your life—big or small—in which following Jesus will require courage, truth, or sacrifice for you?

5. In Romans 8, Paul says present suffering can't compare with the future glory that's coming. How might this perspective strengthen someone who is trying to live under Jesus' authority when it feels costly or unpopular?

DAY 5

WRAP-UP

Use this time to go back and complete any of the study and reflection questions from previous days that you were unable to finish. Make a note of any revelations you've had and reflect on any growth or personal insights you've gained.

Read chapters 10–11 in *The Missing Messiah* before the next group session. Use the space provided to make note of anything in those chapters that stands out to you or encourages you.

SESSION 6

FOLLOWING THE MESSIAH TOGETHER

SESSION 6

GROUP STUDY

WELCOME

There's a profound difference between knowing about Jesus and actually following him. You can master Christian doctrine, study biblical history, and even enter professional ministry without ever truly making Jesus your Rabbi—the one you apprentice under, learn from, and imitate in every area of life.

In first-century Judaism, a rabbi wasn't simply a teacher who passed along information. He was a master who taught his disciples an entire way of life. They didn't only study his words; they watched how he ate, prayed, treated people, handled money, responded to criticism, and lived under pressure. The goal wasn't information but formation—becoming like the rabbi.

When Jesus said, "Follow me," he wasn't inviting people into a religious program; he was calling apprentices into a radically different way of life under the reign of God. He was asking them to pattern everything after him.

Over time, Western Christianity has separated believing in Jesus from following him. We talk about accepting Jesus as Savior while keeping him out of large areas of life—finances, work, relationships, politics, entertainment, and daily priorities. Discipleship is often reduced to agreement rather than transformation.

This week we'll confront an uncomfortable truth: It's possible to admire Jesus without obeying him. Fans know the language, cheer from a distance, and enjoy the benefits. Followers step onto the field and accept the cost.

Jesus never asked for fans. He called for disciples—people who would watch him closely, imitate his ways, adopt his priorities, share his mission, emulate his character, and submit to his authority in every part of life.

Following Jesus was never meant to be done alone. Western individualism promotes the idea that faith is private, something "between me and God." Jesus claimed otherwise. He formed a community, sent disciples out together, taught them to pray, "Our Father," and described them in terms of shared identity.

We can't fully follow Jesus in isolation. We need community to sharpen us, challenge us, encourage us, and keep us honest. Without it, our growth slows, our vision narrows, and our gifts remain underdeveloped.

This final week offers an invitation to move from being fans to being followers—and to recognize that following Jesus means joining his body, the church, where together we represent his continuing presence in the world.

CONNECT

Share one insight or challenge from your personal studies this week. What stood out to you most?

Think of someone who has been a spiritual mentor or example for you. What did you learn from watching their life, not just hearing their words?

WATCH

Watch the session 6 video together. *To access this video session, follow the instructions located at the front of this book.*

NOTES

DISCUSS

1. Invite someone to read 1 John 2:3-6. John says that knowing God is proven not by what we claim but by how we obey and live like Jesus. How does this challenge the modern idea that faith is primarily about believing rather than following?

2. Chapter 10 of *The Missing Messiah* describes the difference between a fan and a follower of Jesus. Fans are enthusiastic admirers who want the benefits without the cost, while followers are apprentices learning to live like their Rabbi. Where do you see yourself on the spectrum of fan to follower? What would need to change for you to move closer to being a true follower?

3. Read Luke 9:23-26 aloud. Jesus says following him requires denying yourself, taking up your cross daily, and being willing to lose your life. How does this radical call to discipleship contrast with the comfortable Christianity that asks little of us? What might taking up your cross daily look like in your life right now?

4. Chapter 11 of *The Missing Messiah* argues that Western individualism has led us to believe we can follow Jesus without the church, but the New Testament shows that discipleship is inherently communal. What do we miss when we try to follow Jesus in isolation?

5. Have someone read Hebrews 10:24-25. The author commands believers not to neglect meeting together but to encourage one another. Beyond just attending church, what would it look like for your group to become the kind of community that truly helps each other follow Jesus?

RESPOND

In this session, we've explored what it means to follow Jesus as our Rabbi and to do so in community. Take a few minutes to reflect using the following passage:

> Follow God's example, therefore, as dearly loved children and walk in the way of love, just as Christ loved us and gave himself up for us as a fragrant offering and sacrifice to God.
> **EPHESIANS 5:1-2**

Paul calls us to imitate God and walk in the way of love, following Christ's example of sacrificial love. In what specific ways is Jesus calling you to love others sacrificially this week?

Where have you been treating discipleship as an individual journey rather than a communal one? What is one step you can take to deepen your commitment to following Jesus with others?

PRAY

Close your time together in prayer.

- Thank Jesus for calling you not just to believe in him but to follow him.
- Confess any areas where you have been a fan rather than a follower.
- Ask him to give you the courage to take up your cross daily and follow him wholeheartedly.
- Pray for your group, that together you would become the kind of community that helps each person follow Jesus more faithfully.

SESSION 6

PERSONAL STUDY

Throughout this week, we'll explore what it means to move from being a fan of Jesus to becoming his follower. We'll examine the Rabbi-disciple relationship, the cost of authentic discipleship, and why following Jesus can't be done alone. Each day you'll be challenged to consider whether you're truly apprenticing under Jesus or simply admiring him from a distance. This final week focuses on obedience and community—what allegiance looks like after the Messiah has been re-recognized and how it's lived out together rather than alone.

As you work through each of these exercises, write down your responses to the questions.

DAY 1

THE RABBI-DISCIPLE RELATIONSHIP

Antonio Stradivari learned to make violins by spending years in the workshop of Nicolò Amati, one of the great luthiers of Cremona, Italy. Young Stradivari didn't just study violin-making techniques—he absorbed Amati's entire approach to the craft. He watched how his master selected wood, noting the grain patterns and listening for the right resonance. He observed the precise pressure of Amati's hands as he carved, the angle of his tools, the patience in his every movement.

Stradivari learned not just what to do but how to think about the work. He absorbed Amati's philosophy of never compromising on quality, treating each instrument as if it would be played for centuries. By the time Stradivari opened his own workshop, people could identify him as Amati's apprentice just by examining his violins. His instruments reflected his master's values, standards, and approach.

Eventually, Stradivari surpassed even his master. Today, Stradivarius violins are considered the finest ever made, worth millions of dollars.[1] But Stradivari would say he learned by watching Amati work, by imitating him until the master's way of craftsmanship became his own.

This is what Jesus meant when he said, "Follow me."

He wasn't inviting people to attend lectures on theology. He was calling them into an intensive apprenticeship in which they learned not just what he taught but how he lived. They watched how he prayed, treated outcasts, responded to criticism, handled power, and loved enemies. They observed him until his way of being in the world became their way.

John captures this idea perfectly: "Whoever claims to live in him must live as Jesus did" (1 John 2:6). Not that his followers must quote what Jesus said or must believe what Jesus believed. They must *live* as Jesus did. Following Jesus means becoming his apprentice, absorbing his way of life so thoroughly that people recognize you as his disciple by watching how you live.

The question isn't whether you know about Jesus. The question is this: Are you becoming like him?

READ AND RESPOND

Read 1 John 2:3-6; 1 Corinthians 11:1; 1 Peter 2:21; Matthew 11:28-30.

1. John says that truly knowing God is proven by obeying his commands and living as Jesus lived. How does this passage challenge the idea that discipleship is primarily about correct beliefs rather than Christlike living?

2. Both Paul and Peter call believers to imitate and follow the example of Jesus (see 1 Corinthians 11:1; 1 Peter 2:21). What does it mean for you to follow in his steps, imitating Christ in practical, everyday ways?

3. Think about someone whose life reflects Jesus in a way that inspires you. What specific qualities or habits do you see in them that you want to develop in your own life? How might you intentionally learn from their example?

4. In the right column, indicate whether what was true of Jesus is also true of you:

True of Jesus	True of me?
Prioritized prayer	
Lived in community	
Cared for the sick	
Reached out to the lonely	
Preached the good news	
Honored the Sabbath	
Knew God's Word	
Loved sacrificially	

Looking at this list, where is the gap between Jesus' life and yours the widest?

What's one specific step you could take this week to close that gap?

5. Read Matthew 11:28-30. Jesus invites us to take his yoke and learn from him. In traditional agricultural, a yoke connects two animals so they can work together, with the experienced one training the inexperienced. How does this image help you understand what it means to be Jesus' disciple?

DAY 2

THE COST OF FOLLOWING JESUS

Jim Elliot was a missionary who, along with four friends, attempted to reach the Waorani people (then called the Auca) in Ecuador's rainforest. The Waorani were known for extreme violence, having killed every outsider who entered their territory. Elliot and his team knew the risks. They spent months preparing, learning the language, and making friendly contact from their airplane.

On January 8, 1956, the five men landed on a beach along the Curaray River. The Waorani appeared, and for a brief moment, contact seemed peaceful. Then spears flew. All five missionaries were killed. Elliot was twenty-eight years old, married less than three years, with a ten-month-old daughter.

Before his death, Elliot had written in his journal: "He is no fool who gives what he cannot keep to gain what he cannot lose." He understood that following Jesus isn't about comfort, safety, or even survival. It's about allegiance to a King worth dying for.

The even more remarkable part of the story came later. Elliot's widow, Elisabeth, along with the sister of another slain missionary, eventually went to live among the Waorani. They learned the language, shared their lives, and told the story of Jesus. Within years, the very men who had killed the missionaries became followers of Christ.[2]

Jesus never hid the price tag of following him, saying, "Whoever wants to be my disciple must deny themselves and take up their cross daily and follow me" (Luke 9:23). Taking up a cross wasn't a metaphor for minor inconvenience—it was an image of execution. Jesus was saying, "Following me will cost you everything."

Most people want the benefits without the cost. They want forgiveness without repentance. Peace without sacrifice. Heaven without surrender. They want to be fans who cheer from the stands but never enter the game.

Here's the question: Has following Jesus cost you anything? If your bank account, calendar, relationships, and lifestyle look identical to those who don't follow Jesus, are you really following him? Or are you just someone who signed up but never showed up?

READ AND RESPOND

Read Luke 9:23-26; Matthew 7:21-23; John 3:1-21.

1. Jesus says following him requires self-denial, taking up a cross daily, and being willing to lose your life. What do you think Jesus means by denying yourself? Where do you need to deny yourself so you can more fully follow him?

2. In Matthew 7, Jesus warns that many will claim him as Lord but will not enter the Kingdom because they didn't do the Father's will. How does this passage challenge the idea that simply believing in Jesus is enough?

3. Why do you think Nicodemus came to Jesus at night? (See John 3:1-2.) What might he have been afraid of losing? In what ways are you tempted to follow Jesus "at night" rather than publicly?

4. Take an honest inventory: Has following Jesus cost you anything? Consider your finances, time, relationships, reputation, comfort, and career. If it hasn't cost you anything, or if it hasn't cost you much, what might this reveal about how wholeheartedly you're following him?

5. Complete this sentence: "If I truly made Jesus my Rabbi and followed him in every area of my life, the thing that would scare me most is . . ."

DAY 3

JESUS AS LORD OF EVERYTHING

Most of us don't reject Jesus' authority outright—we manage it.

We would never say that Jesus *isn't* Lord, but we might say it indirectly with our lives. Maybe we trust him with our forgiveness but not our finances. With eternity but not our time. With church but not work. With prayer but not power, politics, or priorities.

The result is a faith that feels sincere but remains selective.

In the Gospels, Jesus never allowed this kind of partial allegiance. When he called people to follow him, he didn't ask them to add him to an already full life. He asked them to reorder everything around him. Fishermen left their nets. A tax collector abandoned his booth. Others walked away because the cost was too high. Jesus never chased them down to negotiate terms.

That's because discipleship isn't about agreement; it's about *authority*.

Paul makes this explicit in Romans 12:1 when he urges believers to offer their bodies as living sacrifices. Not just their beliefs. Not just their private spirituality. Their bodies—their actions, habits, choices, relationships, and rhythms. Following Jesus isn't confined to what we think; it governs how we live.

This confronts one of the most common distortions of modern Christianity: the idea that Jesus can be Savior without being Lord. We want his grace without his governance. His comfort without his commands. His promises without his interference.

But Jesus doesn't present himself as a consultant. He presents himself as King.

That's why Paul writes in Colossians 3 that Christ isn't only the source of salvation but "your life" (verse 4). When Jesus is Lord, there's no drawer labeled "personal," "private," or "off-limits." There are no neutral zones. Everything belongs to him because everything comes from him.

This doesn't mean following Jesus makes life smaller or more restrictive. It means life finally has a center strong enough to hold it together. When Jesus is Lord of everything, there is coherence instead of fragmentation, freedom instead of fear, direction instead of drift.

The real question of discipleship isn't whether Jesus fits somewhere in your life; it's whether your life is being reshaped around him. Because Jesus doesn't ask for part of you. He asks for all of you—and offers real life in return.

READ AND RESPOND

Read Colossians 3:1-17; James 2:14-26.

1. In Colossians 3, Paul says our lives are now "hidden with Christ" and that Christ is "your life." What do you think it looks like, day-to-day, for Jesus to be your life rather than just an important part of your life?

2. Paul tells believers to put to death some patterns and to clothe ourselves with new ones. What might it look like for you to intentionally take something off or put something on in response to this passage in Colossians?

3. Chapter 10 of *The Missing Messiah* includes a "drawers" metaphor to help us think about the different areas of our lives. Label each "drawer" in the chart with a different area of your life. Put a checkmark next to areas where Jesus has full access. Put an *X* next to drawers where you're keeping him out. Put a question mark next to areas that fall somewhere in between.

My Life		

What would it look like to give Jesus full access to the drawer(s) marked with an *X*?

4. James argues that faith without works is dead and that genuine faith always produces action. How does this passage challenge the idea that all you have to do to be a Christian is believe in Jesus?

5. James says faith is made complete by what it does. What's one concrete action that would strengthen or "complete" your faith right now (see verse 22)?

DAY 4

FOLLOWING JESUS TOGETHER

Aron Ralston was an experienced climber who went hiking alone in Utah's Bluejohn Canyon in April 2003. He didn't tell anyone where he was going. When an eight-hundred-pound boulder shifted and pinned his right arm against the canyon wall, no one knew where to look for him.

For six days, Ralston tried everything to free himself. He chipped at the boulder with a pocketknife. He rigged a pulley system. He rationed his water and energy bars. Nothing worked. The boulder wouldn't budge. On the sixth day, dehydrated and delirious, Ralston realized he had two choices: amputate his own arm or die there.

Using a dull multi-tool, he broke his arm bones and cut through his tissue. The process took over an hour. After freeing himself, he rappelled down a sixty-five-foot cliff and hiked seven miles before rescuers found him. He survived, but barely. Later, Ralston admitted that going alone without telling anyone was his biggest mistake. He knew that if he'd told someone, search and rescue would have found him.[3]

Following Jesus alone is like hiking a dangerous canyon solo. You might make progress for a while. You may feel independent and self-sufficient. But eventually you'll face obstacles you can't overcome without help, dangers you didn't see coming, and problems that require someone else to notice you're missing.

Paul understood this. He described the church as a body: "Just as a body, though one, has many parts, but all its many parts form one body, so it is with Christ" (1 Corinthians 12:12). A severed arm can't function. A disconnected foot can't walk. Every part needs the body.

Without community, we lack spiritual endurance. There's no one to encourage us through hard seasons. We become self-deceived—there's no one to lovingly confront our blind spots. We develop theological blinders—our understanding gets filtered through our limited perspective. We miss our purpose—our gifts remain dormant without a body to serve.

Most importantly, we can't fully know Jesus on our own. The mercy giver shows us Jesus' compassion. The justice seeker reveals Jesus' righteousness. The generous giver displays Jesus' sacrificial love. Together, we see a fuller picture of who Jesus is.

You can't follow Jesus solo. The path is too difficult, the journey too dangerous. We need each other—not because it's nice but because we literally can't make it alone.

READ AND RESPOND

Read 1 Corinthians 12:12-27; Hebrews 10:23-25; Acts 2:42-47.

1. Paul uses the body metaphor to describe why we need each other. According to 1 Corinthians 12, what are the dangers of trying to follow Jesus in isolation? What do we miss when we are disconnected from the body?

2. In Hebrews 10:23-25, we're commanded to not neglect meeting together and to encourage one another, especially as "the Day" approaches. Why is community essential, according to this passage? What would it cost you to prioritize consistent community with other believers?

3. Acts 2:42-47 describes the communal life of the early church—sharing possessions, eating together, meeting in homes, and caring for those in need. How does this picture of radical community challenge typical modern Christianity? What would it look like to recover a portion of this kind of shared life?

4. Chapter 11 of *The Missing Messiah* argues that without community, we develop blind spots, lack accountability, and can't fully know Jesus. Where have you seen these dangers play out—either in your own life or in the lives of others who tried to follow Jesus alone?

5. Reflect on your current experience of Christian community. Put an *X* on the following spectrum indicating where you are now:

Completely isolated — Deeply connected

What steps can you take to move deeper into community so you can more fully follow Jesus and experience the life he has for you?

DAY 5

WRAP-UP

Use this time to go back and complete any of the study and reflection questions from previous days that you were unable to finish. Make a note of any revelations you've had and reflect on any growth or personal insights you've gained.

A FINAL WORD

FOLLOWING THE MESSIAH FORWARD

Over the last six weeks, you've traced a story that began long before Jesus was born and stretches far beyond your own life. You've seen how the Messiah was promised, anticipated, misunderstood, and ultimately revealed—and how Jesus exceeded expectations, not by conforming to what people wanted but by being exactly who God sent him to be.

Following the Messiah is not a onetime decision. It's a lifelong journey, a daily orientation of your life. It means bringing every part of who you are—your work, relationships, ambitions, fears, and hopes—under his lordship. It means trading the comfort of a customized Jesus for the challenge and beauty of the real one.

You may not have all your questions answered. You may still feel tension between what Jesus calls you to and what culture affirms. The world will continue to offer a more "manageable" version of Jesus—a Savior who blesses your life but doesn't reorder it. When you feel that tension, remember that it's not a failure of faith. It's often the place where faith deepens.

So keep going.

Keep returning to Scripture.

Keep examining your assumptions.

Keep gathering with others who will challenge and encourage you.

Keep allowing the Messiah to remain at the center rather than on the margins.

The Messiah you've rediscovered is more demanding than the Jesus our culture prefers. But he is also more glorious, more satisfying, and far more worthy of following.

May you follow him with your whole life—and never settle for anything less than the real, risen, reigning King.

NOTES

SESSION 1: RECOVERING THE REAL MESSIAH

1. David Batty, "Mona Lisa: The Early Years? Art World Split over Leonardo da Vinci 'Work'," *The Guardian*, September 26, 2012, https://www.theguardian.com/artanddesign/2012/sep/26/mona-lisa-teenage-painting-art; "The Mona Lisa," Museo del Prado, accessed April 1, 2026, https://www.museodelprado.es/en/the-collection/art-work/the-mona-lisa/80c9b279-5c80-4d29-b72d-b19cdca6601c.
2. Geoff Herbert, "New Dictionary Definition of 'Literally' Will Literally Make Your Head Explode," Syracuse.com, August 14, 2013, https://www.syracuse.com/news/2013/08/literally_definition_dictionary_wrong_english_languageyour_head_explode.html.
3. See Brittani Barger, "A Look Back on King Tupou VI's Coronation," *Royal Central*, March 18, 2022, https://royalcentral.co.uk/international/a-look-back-on-king-tupou-vis-coronation-173962/; "Tongan King Crowned in Traditional Ceremony," i24NEWS, July 4, 2015, https://www.i24news.tv/en/news/international/asia-pacific/77141-150704-tongan-king-crowned-in traditional-ceremony.
4. C. S. Lewis, *Mere Christianity* (HarperOne, 2001), 136–137.
5. Augustine, *Confessions*, trans. Henry Chadwick (Oxford University Press, 2008), 3.
6. Billy Wright, "Selfie Editing: The Most Popular Apps for Brits!," *How to Kill an Hour*, August 19, 2020, https://www.howtokillanhour.com/gadgets-tech/selfie-editing-the-most-popular-apps-for-brits.
7. City University London, "90% of Young Women Report Using a Filter or Editing Their Photos Before Posting," Science Daily, March 8, 2021, https://www.sciencedaily.com/releases/2021/03/210308111852.htm.

SESSION 2: THE MORPHING MESSIAH

1. Karen Juanita Carrillo, "How Hernán Cortés Conquered the Aztec Empire," History, May 28, 2025, https://www.history.com/articles/hernan-cortes-conquered-aztec-empire.
2. Matthew Restall, *Seven Myths of the Spanish Conquest* (Oxford University Press, 2003), 97–98.

3. David Mikkelson, "Did the Chevrolet Nova Fail to Sell in Spanish-Speaking Countries?" Snopes, April 2, 1999, https://www.snopes.com/fact-check/chevrolet-nova-name-spanish/.
4. Saheli Sukhwal, "6 Marketing Translation Fails That Cost Millions!," Translate by Humans, June 9, 2023, https://translatebyhumans.com/6-marketing-translation-fails-that-cost-millions/.
5. Megan Ziegler, "The Best Super Bowl Commercial Ever: Apple's Macintosh in 1984," Fox 9, February 9, 2025, https://www.fox9.com/news/1984-apple-super-bowl-commercial.
6. Leon Festinger et al., *When Prophecy Fails* (University of Minnesota Press, 1956); Jennifer Kretchmar, "Cognitive Dissonance Theory," EBSCO, 2021, https://www.ebsco.com/research-starters/social-sciences-and-humanities/cognitive-dissonance-theory.
7. "Spanish Fresco Restoration Botched by Amateur," BBC News, August 23, 2012, https://www.bbc.com/news/world-europe-19349921; Sophie Handler, "Grotesque Irreverence: The Transformation of 'Ecce Homo,'" *Sequitur* 2, no. 2 (2016), https://www.bu.edu/sequitur/2016/04/29/handler-ecce/.

SESSION 3: DISCOVERING THE MESSIAH

1. For an overview of the discovery, dating, and contents of the Dead Sea Scrolls, see the "Learn About the Scrolls," The Leon Levy Dead Sea Scrolls Digital Library, Israel Antiquities Authority, accessed March 5, 2026, https://www.deadseascrolls.org.il/home; García Martínez and Tigchelaar, *The Dead Sea Scrolls: A New Translation*; and the British Library, "What Are the Dead Sea Scrolls?"
2. "Eisenhower's Two D-Day Messages," *Prologue* 36, no. 2 (2004): https://www.archives.gov/publications/prologue/2004/summer/ike-two-d-day-messages.
3. United States Holocaust Memorial Museum, "Lucien-Louis Bunel," Holocaust Encyclopedia, accessed March 27, 2025, https://encyclopedia.ushmm.org/content/en/id-card/lucien-louis-bunel.
4. Andreas Kranebitter, ed., *Memorial Book for the Dead of the Mauthausen Concentration Camp and Its Subcamps Volume 1: Commentaries and Biographies* (New Academic Press, 2016), 164–165.
5. Read more at United States Holocaust Memorial Museum, "Father Jacques," Holocaust Encyclopedia, accessed March 5, 2026, https://encyclopedia.ushmm.org/content/en/article/father-jacques.
6. Peter W. Stoner, "The Christ of Prophecy," chap. 3 in *Science Speaks: Scientific Proof of the Accuracy of Prophecy and the Bible* (Moody Press, 1963), 100–107.

SESSION 4: THE MESSIAH NO ONE SAW COMING

1. C.S. Lewis, *Mere Christianity* (HarperOne, 2001), 52.
2. "Strong's G2320—*Theotēs*," Blue Letter Bible, accessed March 27, 2026, https://www.blueletterbible.org/lexicon/g2320/kjv/tr/0-1/.

SESSION 5: THE COMEBACK THAT PROVED HIS MESSIAHSHIP

1. "Tacoma Narrows Bridges," American Society of Civil Engineers, accessed March 11, 2026, https://www.asce.org/about-civil-engineering/history-and-heritage/historic-landmarks/tacoma-narrows-bridges/; "Suspension Bridge," *Nova*, PBS, updated October 2000, https://www.pbs.org/wgbh/nova/bridge/meetsusp.html#clips.

2. Frances Wood, *China's First Emperor and His Terracotta Warriors* (St. Martin's Press, 2008).
3. Ben Pimlott, *The Queen: Elizabeth II and the Monarchy* (HarperCollins, 2001), 207–220.
4. Ferdinand Schlingensiepen, *Dietrich Bonhoeffer 1906–1945: Martyr, Thinker, Man of Resistance*, trans. Isabel Best (T&T Clark, 2010).
5. Dietrich Bonhoeffer, *The Cost of Discipleship*, rev. ed. (Macmillan, 1959), 36–37.

SESSION 6: FOLLOWING THE MESSIAH TOGETHER

1. Historical accounts of Antonio Stradivari's apprenticeship under Nicolò Amati are documented in museum collections and scholarship on Cremonese violin making. See also Wendy Powers, "Violin Makers: Nicolò Amati (1596–1684) and Antonio Stradivari (1644–1737)," The Metropolitan Museum of Art, October 1, 2003, https://www.metmuseum.org/essays/violin-makers-nicolo-amati-1596-1684-and-antonio-stradivari-1644-1737; Stewart Pollens, *Stradivari* (Cambridge University Press, 2010).
2. Elisabeth Elliot, *Through Gates of Splendor* (Tyndale, 1981), 172–256.
3. Aron Ralston, *Between a Rock and a Hard Place* (Atria Books, 2004).

ABOUT THE AUTHORS

Kyle Idleman is a bestselling author and the senior pastor at Southeast Christian Church in Louisville, Kentucky, one of the largest churches in America. Kyle is the author of *Not a Fan*, *One at a Time*, *The End of Me*, *Gods at War*, *Grace Is Greater*, and *Don't Give Up*. Kyle's favorite thing to do is to hang out with the love of his life, DesiRae. They have four children: MacKenzie, Morgan, Macy, and Kael.

Mark E. Moore is the bestselling author of *Core 52* and the teaching pastor at Christ's Church of the Valley in Peoria, Arizona, one of the fastest growing and most dynamic churches in America. He previously spent two decades as a New Testament professor at Ozark Christian College. His life's passion is to make Scripture accessible and relevant to people trying to make sense of Christianity. Mark and his wife, Barbara, live in Peoria.